# American Politics and the Jewish Community

## The Jewish Role in American Life

An Annual Review of the Casden Institute for the
Study of the Jewish Role in American Life

# American Politics and the Jewish Community

## The Jewish Role in American Life

### An Annual Review of the Casden Institute for the Study of the Jewish Role in American Life

## *Volume 11*

Bruce Zuckerman, *Editor*

Dan Schnur, *Guest Editor*

Lisa Ansell, *Associate Editor*

Published by the Purdue University Press for
the USC Casden Institute for the Study of the
Jewish Role in American Life

*Production Editor*, Marilyn Lundberg

*Cover photo:*
The delicate balance between Jewish and American identity is reflected in this photo-
graph of a Jewish citizen in front of the US flag by Middle Eastern photographer Selim
Aksan.
*Courtesy of iStockphoto contributor selimaksan (File #13030976).*

Cloth ISBN 978-1-55753-659-4
ePDF ISBN 978-1-61249-299-5
ePUB ISBN 978-1-61249-300-8
ISSN 1934-7529

Published by Purdue University Press
West Lafayette, Indiana
www.thepress.purdue.edu
pupress@purdue.edu

Printed in the United States of America.

For subscription information,
call 1-800-247-6553

# Contents

# Foreword

It's hardly surprising. In the course of putting together, in collaboration with our various guest editors, this *Annual Review* of the Casden Institute for the Study of the Jewish Role in American Life, we have focused on a broad variety of topics, and areas of research and interest—indeed, from my standpoint, the broader the better. Yet in many if not most of the articles we have published there has tended to be an underlying theme that always seems to be there. Politics. As I said, it is hardly surprising that most everything worthy of consideration about Jews in America has a political dimension. Arguably, politics is a kind of black hole for American Jews, around which the entire galaxy of all their conceptual and cultural endeavors inevitably turns.

Considering this, perhaps it *is* surprising that through the first ten volumes of the *Annual Review* we have not yet placed our central focus on politics in an American Jewish context *per se*. This Volume 11, entitled *American Politics and the Jewish Community*, intends to address this oversight, and we could have no better choice for doing this than our guest-editor for this collection of essays, Dan Schnur. Prof. Schnur looks at American politics from an especially appropriate vantage point here at the University of Southern California, in his role as the first director of the Jesse M. Unruh Institute of Politics in the David Dornsife College of Letters Arts & Sciences. The Casden and Unruh Institutes have formed a natural and close alliance that has resulted in a number of collaborative projects over the years through which we have creatively considered how Jewish American culture and politics so easily yet intricately superimpose upon one another. So when we decided to focus on American politics and its relationship to the American Jewish community, it was both a wise and easy decision to choose Prof. Schnur to be our guide. And, as you read the essays that follow, you will discover what a fine guide he has proven to be. So I want to take this opportunity to thank him for the many hours of effort he put into making this such an interesting and intriguing volume.

In the final analysis, politics often comes down to a matter of numbers. That is, political decisions are made or, perhaps better, affirmed, depending on how many people at a given time vote for this-or-that candidate for office and/or in support of a given agenda (overt or hidden) that given candidates represent. So Prof. Schnur has called upon a number of his colleagues in order to have them report on and interpret the implications of the demographics for Jewish voters in national (that is presidential and congressional) elections from the post-World War II period right up to the present day. Indeed, some of the statistics employed below come from surveys that encompass the 2012 national election and which have only just now been published in 2013.

What they show is a remarkably consistent pattern that brings to my mind a paraphrase of the question annually posed at Passover (here, with slight political adjustment): "Why is the Jewish-American voting-bloc different from all other national voting blocs?" Or to put this another way, we might well ask: "Why does there seem to be no Republican elephant in most Jewish living rooms?" In one way or another, these two issues are well addressed in the various essays that comprise this *Annual Review*, and I have no doubt that our readers will enjoy assaying how and why the numbers crunch so intriguingly as shown in the studies, below.

As always is the case, there are a number of people that I gratefully acknowledge for making this *Annual Review* possible. Charles Watkinson and Katherine Purple at Purdue University Press have been unusually patient with us this time around. This volume came together a bit more slowly than one would have wished, and I am truly appreciative of their maintaining a consistently tolerant and encouraging attitude rather than (as I am sure they must have felt from time to time) conveying their exasperation. On our end, Lisa Ansell, Associate Director of the Casden Institute, and Marilyn J. Lundberg, who has done her always meticulous job of production editing for our *Annual Reviews*, made sure that everything fell into place. I really do not know how I would manage without them. The support of the Dean of Dornsife College, Steve Kay, and of the University Provost, Beth Garrett and, of course, our University President, C. L. Max Nikias, continues to be essential to the overall success of the Casden Institute, in general, and this volume, in particular. Most of all, our stalwart friends and supporters, Ruth Ziegler and Alan Casden have our thanks and appreciation, for without them, there would be no Casden Institute.

This last year has been one of departures. We very much regret that our long time friend, advisor and mentor, Susan Wilcox, has decided to leave her position as Associate Dean for Dornsife Development to take another position outside the University. Her successor in Dornsife Development David

Eshaghpour has already proven to be a fine colleague who has gone out of his way to show us that the welfare of the Casden Institute is his high priority.

Far more sad for all of us is the death during this last year of one of the most constant supporters of the Casden Institute, Carmen Warschaw. I am now especially grateful that we had an opportunity to dedicate a previous volume of this *Annual Review* two years ago in her honor, so we could publicly acknowledge to her—and in memory of her late husband Louis—how important their commitment to Jewish studies in America has meant to USC. It is gratifying that the Warschaw family, and in particular Carmen's and Louis' daughter Hope, continue to play an active role in shaping the Casden Institute's future endeavors, especially in regard to the Warschaw Lectures, named in Carmen's and Louis' honor.

The most prestigious and venerable lecture series at USC focused on Jewish culture is the Nemer Lecture—older by a number of years than even the Casden Institute, itself. This lecture was named after Jerry Nemer and funded by the Nemer family in order to ensure that USC will remain engaged in a consideration of Jewish thought, thanks to the stellar lecturers that have come to USC, year after year. It was always my particular pleasure to sit next to the matriarch of the Nemer family, Harriett, Jerry's wife, during each and every Nemer Lecture. She would often put her hand on my arm and squeeze it when she thought the lecturer made a particularly telling point. I knew how good a lecture was based on how many squeezes I got.

Harriet died during the past year and this will be the first Nemer Lecture where her seat in the front row (she always insisted on being in the front row) will be vacant. But, of course, her memory will always be an essential part of the Nemer Lecture, just as Jerry's memory has been before her. And I have no doubt that her children and grandchildren, always present at the Nemer with her, will continue to be present as we celebrate her and Jerry's memory in the best way possible—through the presentations that portray for us just how important has been the Jewish contribution to the life of USC.

We are therefore very pleased to dedicate this *Annual Review* to her memory and to the memory and legacy of her husband Jerry.

Bruce Zuckerman, *Myron and Marian Casden Director*

# Editorial Introduction

## *Dan Schnur, Guest Editor*

Anyone who would pick up a book with the title *American Politics and the Jewish Community* is almost certainly interested not only in the American Jewish political experience but is also an informed observer of our political system overall. As a result, you are likely to be as alarmed as I am about the growing polarization and hyper-partisanship that has crippled our democratic process. You are just as likely to understand why the continued gridlock caused by two political parties beholden to their respective ideological bases will prevent our government from adequately addressing our society's most pressing challenges. Whether you prefer to direct blame at conservatives or liberals, at Tea Partiers or Occupiers, makes little difference. Every day, we see growing evidence that American politics is broken.

What may be less apparent is why this political paralysis is so relevant not only to the ongoing debates about taxes and health care, about education and immigration, but why it plays such an important role in a more specific conversation about Jewish voters and American politics. Because the Democratic Party enjoys such an overwhelming advantage in terms of support from this country's Jewish community, it's fairly easy to disregard the immediate consequences of political polarization for Jewish voters. But anyone who watched an American President in the fall of 2012 unsuccessfully attempt to muster support in Congress for aggressive action in Syria that would have served both US and Israeli security interests should understand that the veto power that the most conservative of Republicans and most liberal of Democrats wield over their respective parties can immobilize our government from necessary action on both domestic and foreign policy. Barack Obama and Republican congressional leaders were both outflanked by the bases of their parties, suggesting that their defeat on Syria was not an outlier but an indicator of future difficulties in confronting a growing isolationist sentiment in this country.

There was once a time when Democrats such as Scoop Jackson and Republicans like Dick Lugar could form a bulwark at the center of the political debate on behalf of American global leadership. But that type of bipartisanship has all but disappeared, replaced by two parties whose members have the marked tendency to occupy ideological cul-de-sacs at the far reaches of the political spectrum. The hostility that many Republicans demonstrate toward immigration reform, that many Democrats exhibit toward expanded free trade opportunities, and that the bases of both parties show toward assertive diplomatic and military engagement conspire to shrink the US role on a global stage. Growing isolationist tendencies in this country and a diminished voice for American engagement involvement can not be a good thing for Israel in an increasingly restive Middle East, flanked by an increasingly diffident Europe, and confronting an increasingly mercenary China and Russia. More than ever, Israel needs a reliable and assertive ally, and an inward-looking United States is less than ideally equipped to play that role.

This is not to suggest that Israel is the dominant issue in American Jewish political thought. In fact, as several articles in this volume note, public opinion polling suggests just the opposite, that Jewish voters in this country are far more likely to cast their ballots on domestic policy matters than on issues related to Israel and the Middle East. These tendencies work strongly in favor of Democratic candidates. Even though most public opinion polls show great reservations among American Jews for President Obama's efforts in this part of the world, those same polls tend to show a strong prioritization on domestic policy matters among Jewish voters. And while Jews may slightly prefer a more redistributionist approach on economic issues, it is clear that social and cultural matters—grounded in both policy and attitude—have a much greater impact on their voting tendencies.

In various ways, our authors point to the discomfort that most Jewish voters feel, when confronted with an agenda advocating for an assertive religious presence in the public square. Jews are not anti-religion, of course, but many intuitively feel threatened when a religious majority begins to stake out policy turf in an aggressive manner. It's doubtful that many evangelical or fundamentalist Christians have ill will toward Jews on a personal basis, but a policy agenda that even inadvertently implies a lack of tolerance or respect for other religious faiths is, from an American Jewish perspective, problematic. Conversely, a Reform and Conservative Jewish community that strongly favors reproductive rights, gun control and marriage equality will have little interest in culturally and socially conservative issue priorities.

If Israel were the most important policy priority for American Jewish voters, then Republicans might be in a better position to compete for their votes. Many US Jews were troubled by Obama's early insistence on a settlement freeze. They also took umbrage at his use of the emotionally charged term "occupation" in reference to the Israeli military presence in Palestinian territory in a seminal speech in Cairo during his first months in office. The ongoing coolness between Obama and Israeli Prime Minister Benjamin Netanyahu has not helped matters, nor has the administration's emphasis on diplomacy over military engagement, when it comes to Iran's nuclear facilities.

But while many Jewish Americans might concede that Republicans are more stalwart in their support for Israel's political leadership (a point that Netanyahu strongly implied during the 2012 election), most see the differences between the two parties in shades of gray. The distinctions between Democrats and Republicans on domestic issues, particularly social and cultural matters, are much more stark. The result is an electoral imbalance of such significance that Democratic presidential candidates often win the Jewish vote by larger margins than they do among Hispanic-Americans. Ira Sheskin's chapter, in particular, does an excellent job of outlining the reasons for this trend, although the chapters authored by all four of our academic contributors play a vital role in understanding the American Jewish political landscape.

In the immediate moment, that's a much bigger problem for Republican candidates than for Jewish voters. But the American Jewish community benefits as well from a legitimate competition for their support. Many Jews may doubt that the full-throated support that Republican leaders have demonstrated for Netanyahu's Likud government represents the best path to peace. But they are just as uncomfortable when they see the obvious tensions that have developed between the President of the United States and the Israeli Prime Minister. It's hard to believe that Obama would not have greater motivation to repair that relationship or to take more assertive stances with Syria and Iran, if he felt that there was even the slightest chance of American Jews switching their partisan allegiance.

The cultural divisions that separate Jewish Americans from religious conservatives show little sign of easing. The mutual suspicion and disregard between the two communities that Eric Uslaner outlines in his chapter are a major source of these tensions, and Steven Windmueller does an excellent job of illustrating their historical roots. Sandy Maisel's chapter provides examples of Jewish candidates successfully winning support from non-Jewish voters, noting that these tend to be drawn from more secularly-oriented communities.

The partisan chasm has only deepened in recent years. The nation's political divisions are frequently exaggerated by the drawing of congressional and legislative boundaries that make the vast majority of districts safe for one party or the other. Members of Congress who know they will never be seriously challenged in a general election by a member of the opposing party, but could easily lose their seat as a result of a primary challenge for a more ideologically extreme candidate from their own ranks, have no incentive to look for opportunities to reach across party lines or move toward the center.

But the partisan divide also continues to grow because of the advances in communications technology that allow us to create what the *New York Times* columnist Nicholas Kristof calls "The Me Network." While there's no question that cable television, talk radio, Internet-based tools and social networking empower us as communicators, the ability to construct our own information and opinion environments can also isolate us in a political, social and cultural echo-chamber. If we're not careful, we begin to cut off our exposure to voices that might challenge or question us, and instead rely only on those who would reinforce our existing beliefs and congratulate us for holding them.

Some may indulge their opinions on Fox News, others on MSNBC. Human nature guides us toward radio stations and websites and Facebook pages that offer us reassurance that our opinions are the right ones. But in the process, we quickly arrive at a point where the only time we are ever exposed to someone with whom we disagree is when they are held up as a caricature or an object of ridicule. The result is that our willingness to attempt to bridge ideological, political or cultural differences quickly disappears.

We live in an iPod nation. The challenge is for us to remember to occasionally remove the white plugs from our ears in order to hear what those with whom we disagree are saying. These efforts will not cause legitimate differences to vanish, but they will dramatically increase the possibility of working our collective way past them. American Jews and religious conservatives will never convince each other to renounce long and deeply held positions on social and cultural policy matters, but a more sustained effort to communicate may benefit both communities.

In the interest of full-disclosure, I worked in Republican politics for many years before moving to academia. Like more than twenty percent of my fellow Californians, I am now classified as a No Party Preference voter, registered to vote but with no affiliation to any of the state's political parties. I am for lower taxes and marriage equality. I am tough on crime and I am pro-choice. I believe that a pathway to citizenship is a necessary part of immigration reform and that student test scores are a critical component for teacher evaluations. I believe that the best work gets done when both sides are willing to move closer to midfield in order to find common ground. But I no longer have any vested interest in the success of one party or the other.

However, I am still an American Jew and proudly so. I am a tireless supporter of the state of Israel and advocate strongly and regularly for its safety and security. Both my Jewish homeland and my Jewish faith will benefit immeasurably from greater understanding and greater support from both of this country's major political parties and from our continued and accelerated efforts to bring that understanding to them. I hope the conversation that this book begins can help achieve those goals and that you, as a reader, will find some benefit in what you find in the pages to follow.

---

This volume was originally intended to be a broad and far-reaching examination of the role of the Jewish community in American politics, looking at a range of historical, demographic, cultural and electoral factors to determine why a people who represent only two percent of the nation's politics can have such an outsized impact on that nation's systems of governance and politics. Thanks to a tremendously talented group of contributors, I am confident we have accomplished that goal and I hope that readers will complete this volume with a better understanding of the role that American Jews have played in this country's civic structure. I owe great thanks to Professors Sandy Maisel of Colby College, Ira Sheskin of the University of Miami , Ric Uslaner of the University of Maryland and Steven Windmueller of Hebrew Union College for their outstanding contributions. Their research, their insight and their determination combine to create a tremendously valuable intellectual product.

But it also became very clear that, even as our contributors took to their tasks from a variety of perspectives, that this book would ultimately and perhaps unsurprisingly focus on the specific question of partisan voting behavior. Over and over, we found ourselves back to a discussion as to why the GOP was so noticeably and overwhelmingly absent from the Jewish political and electoral decision-making process.

Although our academic contributors varied in their explanations as to why Jewish voting was so one-sided, there was no disagreement as to the likelihood of this trend continuing through the foreseeable future. As a result,

Casden Institute Director Bruce Zuckerman and I decided we should also include the viewpoints of those who have arrived at a different conclusion. As a
result, we are happy to include essays from longtime Jewish Republican political activist Fred Zeidman, who has written about the roots of his own political
involvement, and Republican Jewish Committee Executive Director Matthew
Brooks, who makes the case as to why Jewish voters should consider supporting his party's candidates. We include these contributions not as an attempt to
change readers' minds about their own political leanings, but rather to present
a full range of insight and analysis from contributors who come to this question from different perspectives. I owe a special thanks to Fred and Matt, both
of whom provided an immeasurably valuable perspective to a discussion of
critical importance. The fact that I no longer share a partisan affiliation with
them in no way diminishes my tremendous respect for them, and I am extremely grateful for their willingness to participate in our work.

We're also extremely excited to include an essay from Dennis Ross, the
long-time diplomat and advisor to American presidents of both parties. There
is no one with a deeper, broader and better understanding of the challenges we
face in the Middle East than Dennis, and there is no one who has given more
of himself to lay the groundwork for peace between Israel and its neighbors
than Dennis. He is a genuine American hero for the work that he has done and
continues to do, and I am proud to call him a friend. He may also be one of the
busiest people on the planet, and the fact that he was willing to take time away
from his travel, his speaking, his writing and his other obligations to contribute
his thoughts on the role of Israel in the American political debate is an act of
generosity that I will not forget. His contribution is of immense value to our
overall goals for this project, and this volume would be lacking without it.

I am hugely grateful to both Bruce Zuckerman, the Director of the
Casden Institute and the *real* editor of this book, as well as Lisa Ansell, the
Casden Institute's Deputy Director and resident force of nature. I have been
honored to collaborate with them on programming on the USC campus and
was tremendously flattered when they asked me to serve as guest editor for this
volume. The University of Southern California and the Jewish community are
fortunate to have both Bruce and Lisa for their tireless work on behalf of causes
that are important to so many of us. I know few people who have made such a
significant contribution to our campus and tour community. I must also thank
Alan Casden, whose vision and generosity have not only made this book series
and the Institute itself possible, but whose commitment to Jewish life has made
a profound difference in the lives of too many people to count.

In addition, my colleagues at the Unruh Institute of Politics—who work harder than anyone on the USC campus to help our students learn the value of public service—deserve my thanks as well: Kerstyn Olson, Roslyn Warren, Andrenna Hidalgo, Laura Hill, Thuy Huynh, Carly Armstrong, Jodi Epstein, Luca Servodio, Art Auerbach, Claire Han, Bret Van den Bos, Jeannine Yutani and a battalion of student workers, all of whose dedication toward our goals allow me to take on projects like this one and provide USC students with the tools to make a difference in their communities and in our world.

My deepest thanks as well to Dean Howard Gillman, who hired me as the Director of the Unruh Institute, and Dean Steve Kay, whose ongoing support has allowed my colleagues and I to accomplish more than we ever could have imagined. There are too many others at USC whose guidance and encouragement have been of immense benefit to me to mention, but I am especially grateful to our Provost, Elizabeth Garrett, and University Fellow Geoff Cowan.

Finally, I hope you'll indulge me briefly while I thank the people in my life without whose support I could have never taken on this project or successfully completed it. Though they are no longer with us, the lessons I learned from my great-grandfather Sam Stahl, my grandparents Pearl and Nathan Berkowitz, and my mother Phyllis about the importance of our Jewish community and the state of Israel are the foundation for my commitment to these causes. My father and brother, Robert and Jonathan, have been the two pillars in my life for as long as I can remember, and I cannot imagine any success that I have achieved occurring without having them in my life. I have too many aunts and uncles and cousins who have been there for me when I needed them, and I wish there were enough space on these pages to list every member of my extended family who has guided me and shaped me.

And then there is my wife Cecile, who is simply the most important person in my life and the most wonderful person in the world. Cecile and Rob and Tessa have changed my life and made it whole. It would take another volume to express to them how much they mean to me.

# Introduction: Where Does Israel Fit In?

## *Dennis Ross*

The theme of where Israel fits into American politics and policy tends to produce debates that typically generate more heat than light. Arguments are almost always heavy on assertion and sparse on facts. Yet, as a practitioner of policy on the Middle East in five different administrations and as a political appointee of four Presidents, I have had an interesting vantage point from which to assess this issue.

For one thing, I am struck by the fact that in nearly every administration of which I was a part, Israel figured prominently in the US approach to Middle East policy. For those administrations in which the pursuit of Arab-Israeli peace was the key priority this should come as no surprise. What may come as a surprise is that none of the administrations in which I played a role had a fundamental approach that was decided by political considerations.

In the Arab Middle East, this will come as a surprise because the narrative that has developed over time in most Arab countries is that political considerations drive or determine what the United States does in the Middle East. Similar to the so-called realists in our country who believe that narrow interests like oil should decide our approach to the region, many in the Middle East cannot conceive that US support for Israel could be driven by anything but politics. They argue that our interests should dictate support for the Arabs, not Israel. However, not a single Arab country—even during this period of "awakening"—is characterized by democracy, the rule of law, and the credible separation of legislative, executive and judicial powers. Israel, on the other hand, does enjoy these features, which creates a bond and a set of shared values with the United States.

Historically, Arab leaders were no doubt reluctant to call attention to what Israel shares with the United States; it would be a reminder of what Arab publics lacked. Moreover, it was far easier to try to say that the Americans were governed by their politics and not their interests—and to blame the policies that they did not like on our politics. While it might be understandable for those in the Arab world to try to explain our policy in such a fashion, the "realists" in this country have neither the excuse nor the reason to fixate on politics instead of shared values and interests.

Those who have wanted to attribute our Middle East policy to politics—or more typically to the "Israeli lobby"—have done so largely because they do not like the US approach. They have wanted us to either distance ourselves from or impose greater pressure on Israel. They see the association with Israel as costing us in our relations with Arab countries and believe that we could do much more with them if only we were not saddled with our commitments to Israel or if only the Palestinian conflict no longer existed. Indeed, since Israel's emergence as a state there has been an abiding conventional wisdom among many in the US national security establishment that if only Israel did not complicate our life or if only the Palestinian problem did not exist, our difficulties and the conflicts in the Middle East would disappear.

One can find such views embedded in US administrations going back to the period even before Israel became a state. The opposition of George Marshall and realists such as George Kennan and Loy Henderson to the partition of Palestine and later to our recognition of an Israeli state was based on the presumption that it would cost us our Arab friends and permit the Soviets to exploit Arab anger and gain entrée into the region. Even after the Soviets supported the partition plan in the UN, Kennan and Henderson would write a joint memo in January 1948 arguing for us to reverse US support for partition (United States Department of State). And although President Truman would not reverse our position, he would accept the need to impose an arms embargo shortly after the partition plan was adopted. The US embargo, however, penalized only one side: the Yishuv (the Jewish community in Palestine), because the British were providing arms to Iraq, Transjordan and Egypt—arms which were then supplied to the Arabs of Palestine. Marshall and others resisted political pressure to provide arms to the Yishuv on the grounds that if we provided arms to the Jews, the Arabs would never forgive us and we would lose our position in the Middle East to the Soviets. And, yet when the Soviets provided arms to the Jewish forces in Palestine through the Czechs in April and May of 1948, the sky did not fall. Yet, we still would not end the embargo on arms. That embargo continued even after Israel was declared as a state—and the argument that spawned it failed to be discredited.

It was not until the Kennedy Administration that the United States would begin providing more than small arms to Israel, although President John F. Kennedy faced extensive internal resistance to doing so. Lyndon Johnson would then be the first American President to authorize the transfer of offensive weapons like planes and tanks to Israel. Ironically, it was US military support for Israel—which did not become central until after the 1973 war—that ultimately led Egyptian President Anwar Sadat to see the US as the only possible broker for peace. Only the United States, in his eyes, could affect Israeli policy and permit him to recover Egyptian land.

Rather than preventing ties to the Arab states, then, the US relationship with Israel actually created an incentive for some to turn to us. To be sure, others like the Saudis did feel defensive about their ties to the United States because of our support for Israel. And surely the Saudis, Jordanians and others have consistently complained about Israeli policies and told countless American officials how our support for Israel complicates our position in the area and feeds the anger of the "street" toward the United States. The perceived cost of the US-Israeli relationship—and the consequences for us and the region of not settling the Palestinian conflict—has remained a staple for realists in this country and has been embedded in parts of the national security bureaucracy since Truman's time. Consider that in July of 2013, General James Mattis, recently retired as the head of Central Command, the military command responsible for the greater Middle East, said in a speech in Aspen that our inability to resolve the Palestinian conflict was costing us terribly in the region and preventing the security cooperation we needed with Arab governments (Eran).

For Mattis, the Palestinian issue was at the center of concerns in the Middle East and this was the paramount problem we must solve in the summer of 2013—at a time when the conflict in Syria had already made over one-third of all Syrians refugees and claimed over 100,000 lives; when the Egyptian military had intervened to remove President Morsi and begun a crackdown on the Muslim Brotherhood; when the Iranian nuclear program showed no signs of abating but a new Iranian president had been elected largely because of the pressure of American sanctions; when violence in Iraq, at least in part because of the war in Syria, had returned to the 2008 levels; when the turmoil in Yemen and Libya showed no signs of abating and a political transition in Tunisia was moving in fits and starts. If the Palestinian issue disappeared to tomorrow, it would not alter any of these conflicts or realities in the region.

I don't say this to minimize the value or importance of settling the Israeli-Palestinian conflict. I have spent the last thirty years trying to contribute to resolving that conflict because on its own merits it needs to be resolved and because it is an evocative issue in the region. It certainly affects what key Arab leaders feel they can do with Israel and makes many defensive about their ties to the United States. Not to mention that the Arab publics—having been socialized on hatred of Israel by their governments—have a profoundly negative view of Israel.

But several points should be understood: First, the Saudis and others base their ties to the United States on their needs and priorities and not our relationship with Israel. They have seen us as the guarantor of their security and as long as they perceive this to be the case, will not let their relations with America drop below a certain level. Moreover, even if the Palestinian issue did not exist there would also be a ceiling above which the Saudis and others would not let the relationship go. They want to keep US military presence limited on their soil because they worry that it would be a point of internal destabilization—that al Qaeda, the Muslim Brotherhood, or the Iranians would be sure to try to exploit the appearance of their dependence on us. Second, the region today is consumed by upheaval that is unrelated to the Palestinian issue. The preoccupation is on that upheaval and it will not go away any time soon. Indeed, American problems with the Gulf States today are far more related to their concerns about the US approach to Iran, Syria and Egypt than about Israel. Third, it is the very preoccupation with all other issues that ironically creates space to try to resolve the Israeli-Palestinian conflict at this point—and we are right to try to resolve it lest the current relative stability in the West Bank disappear.

General Mattis' observations remind us that old habits and ways of thinking die hard. Even when the circumstances should dictate otherwise and force us to question our long-standing assumptions, it is hard to give up beliefs that have become cemented over time. Indeed, just as Israel has not undermined our position in the Middle East and US Presidents have actually seen cooperation and sustaining a commitment to Israel to be in our interest, our politics have not mandated our posture in the region.

To be sure, Congress generally has been supportive of Israel even when differences have emerged between American Presidents and their Israeli counterparts over Israeli policies. In order to get the Airborne Warning and Control Systems (AWACS) sale to Saudi Arabia through the Senate, for instance, President Ronald Reagan would say that he "experienced one of his toughest battles of my eight years in Washington" because "Israel had very strong friends in Congress" (Reagan 416). A year later in December 1982, notwithstanding deep differences between the Reagan Administration and Israel over its war in Lebanon, siege of Beirut, and continued presence around the city, Congress approved $250 million in assistance for Israel over the strong opposition of President Reagan and Secretary George Shultz. Where congressional prerogatives are strong—on appropriating money or authorizing arms sales, for instance—administrations have felt the weight of their influence. And, surely congressional attitudes are much more subject to political pressures. But even here, Israel as a brand has credibility in this country. It is seen to embody American values and it is seen as an American friend in a region where there are few who actually do embody our values or can be counted on to consistently support US policies. Even in congressional districts with little or no Jewish presence, there is a tendency to support Israel, and national support for Israel in all polls tends dwarf that of any of the Arab states or polities.

So there is something beyond politics that explains support for Israel in the country and in Congress. That said, congressional support for Israeli policies is more likely to reflect the position of those who are active in the Jewish community than in the executive branch. Here again, however, Congress does not make American foreign or national security policy and congressional positions have not necessarily deterred American Presidents from pursuing what they think our interests require in the Middle East. Indeed, even knowing they might have to expend political capital to overcome potential congressional opposition, Presidents have been willing to do so if they felt our interests in the region required it. And, truth be told, they usually succeeded when they did so.

From the Carter administration's provision of F-15s to Saudi Arabia to the Obama administration's advanced aircraft and helicopter sales to the Saudis, American Presidents have typically prevailed on controversial arms transfers even if, as in Reagan's case, it took some real time and effort—and some understandings and compensation to Israel—to do so.

Even George H. W. Bush, when he opposed Israel's request for $10 billion in loan guarantees in 1991 because of his opposition to Israeli settlement activity and policy, was able to block the Shamir government's request notwithstanding considerable congressional support for it. Ultimately, it is the executive branch that formulates and implements foreign policy and national security; the Congress can affect what Presidents do in foreign policy but clearly do not determine what paths or priorities Presidents adopt.

And, notwithstanding the Walt-Mearsheimer school of realism, every US President for whom I was a political appointee—Reagan, Bush 41, Bill Clinton, and Barak Obama—defined their national security priorities based on what they thought was right and necessary for the country and not what they thought the "lobby" would support or oppose. Their approach to Israel reflected different mindsets: Reagan for instance felt a deep, emotional attachment to Israel but was still prepared to take steps that the Israeli government completely opposed. Indeed, the President decided after the Israeli siege of Beirut and the expulsion of the PLO that the US needed to make a push on peace, and he launched the Reagan Plan—a plan he knew Prime Minister Menachem Begin would oppose. George H. W. Bush, as noted above, opposed loan guarantees to Israel even after Israel absorbed Iraqi SCUD missile attacks during the first Gulf War and acceded to our request not to retaliate lest it put a strain on our coalition and shift the focus in the war. Clinton shared a deep and abiding connection to Israel, and enormous respect for Prime Minister Rabin, but he could also press Israeli Prime Ministers Benjamin Netanyahu and Ehud Barak on the peace issue—a central focus of his Administration. President Obama could go to Saudi Arabia, Egypt, and reach out to the Muslims around the world in a speech in Cairo and not go to Israel as a way of reaching out to Muslims and distancing from Israel given his desire in his first year to demonstrate how different his presidency would be from that of George W. Bush. Later, he would press for President Hosni Mubarak to leave office given a perception that this was the key to managing change in Egypt—a position that Israelis, and the Gulf States, profoundly opposed.

And, of course, George W. Bush did not go to war in Iraq because of Israel. The Israelis felt the threat was Iran and not Iraq and preferred that our focus and efforts at disarmament—whether diplomatic or military—be riveted on the Iranians. But President Bush had a different preoccupation after 9/11.

President Obama and Prime Minister Netanyahu may share a preoccupation with Iran. Indeed, no issue has garnered more time on President Obama's national security agenda than Iran and its nuclear program. In no small part this has been the result of concerns that Israel might launch a military strike otherwise. The Israeli concerns helped create a sense of urgency, but even if Israel were not preoccupied with what it perceives as an existential threat from Iran's having a nuclear weapon, President Obama would still have felt the need to give this issue great priority. His non-proliferation agenda and his genuine fears about the consequences for the Middle East of an Iran nuclear weapons' capability made him believe this was an issue that threatened vital US national security interests. Israel's concerns did not create this priority, even if they added to the urgency with which the Administration formulated its policy. Still, while Obama has agreed with Netanyahu strategically, they have not necessarily agreed on the tactics—with the Israeli prime minister uneasy about what the US might accept as a diplomatic outcome and feeling the need for Iran to be more certain that it would face the use of force if diplomacy failed.

To put all this in perspective: it is not politics that has driven American administrations in their approach to the Middle East and it is certainly not the so-called Israeli lobby that has shaped US foreign policy in the area. American Presidents are keenly aware of what it takes to sustain support for their policies and the closer one gets to presidential elections, the more electoral considerations will be taken into account on *all* issues. That is just as true for domestic policy as it is for foreign policy. It has been good politics to be a friend of Israel for the reasons noted above. But even here, I saw President Clinton, who was passionately committed to the Israeli relationship and to deep strategic cooperation with it, decide to take a step in 1996 that was bound to entail putting some pressure on an Israeli prime minister only two months before his November re-election date. At the time, there was escalating violence between Israelis and Palestinians that had been triggered after the Netanyahu government had acquiesced in a controversial decision by Ehud Olmert, then the Mayor of Jerusalem, to open a tunnel in the Old City. As Clinton's negotiator in the Middle East at the time, I told him that only by calling for a Summit and inviting King Hussein of Jordan, President Mubarak of Egypt, Prime Minister Netanyahu of Israel, and Chairman Yasser Arafat of the Palestinian Authority to the White House would we create an event with enough drama to give everyone a reason to pause and stop the violence—but Prime Minister Netanyahu would inevitably come under the pressure from all those in attendance to do something. All of Clinton's political advisors adamantly were opposed to his calling for the summit, but he went ahead and cast aside the political risks.[1]

Truth be told, given Clinton's identification with Israel, and particularly the connections he forged with the Israeli public in two trips to Israel after the Rabin assassination and three months later when four bombs in nine days threatened to undermine the possibility of peace, it would have been difficult to portray him as soft on Israel. Still, some were tempted to try. More than anyone else, the Israelis have understood the importance of not making Israel a partisan issue in American politics and campaigns. The US relationship with Israel cannot be a Democratic or Republican issue but an American issue. And, in the Congress the bipartisan nature of support for Israel has been overwhelming.

During President Obama's first term, however, there was clearly an effort by some on the Republican side to exploit some of the tensions that emerged in the relationship between the Obama Administration and Israel over the settlement issue. Governor Mitt Romney when he was running for the presidency would later declare that President Obama had "thrown Israel under the bus." He certainly hoped to attract Jewish votes and money—and the disinformation about Obama's policy toward Israel seemed to know no bounds. Criticism of certain administration policies is one thing; trying to say the Democrats and the President were enemies of Israel was something else.

As someone who has worked for Republican and Democratic Presidents alike, and as someone who sees the importance of the US-Israeli relationship to our interests in the Middle East, I was very much against the effort to turn Israel into a political football. No genuine friend of Israel should want that. The fact that policy dictates have guided us in the Middle East will no doubt remain the case and they should. And, so, too, should our approach to Israel be guided by the national interests of the United States and not the narrow interests of those who seek short-term political gain—and whose concerns for Israel are more tactical than strategic.

## Notes

1. Mubarak was the only one invited who did not come, perhaps doubting that Clinton
   would do what was necessary in the meeting given the timing.

## Works Cited

Eran, Oded. "America's Mixed Messages to Israel." *The National Interest* 7 Aug. 2013.
    29 Oct. 2013 <http://nationalinterest.org/commentary/americas-mixed-messages-
    israel-8844>.

Reagan, Ronald. *An American Life*. New York: Simon and Schuster, 1990.

United States Department of State. "Memorandum of the Director of the Policy Planning
    Staff (Kennan) to the Secretary of State [and attached memo]," 20 Jan, 1948. *Foreign
    Relations of the United States, 1948. The Near East, South Asia, and Africa (in Two
    Parts)*. Vol. 5, Part 2. Washington, DC: US Government Printing Office, 1948. 545–
    54. 29 Oct. 2013 <http://images.library.wisc.edu/FRUS/EFacs/1948v05p2/refer-
    ence/frus.frus1948v05p2.i0008.pdf>.

# SECTION ONE

# The Jewish Contract with America

*Steven Windmueller*

INTRODUCTION: DEFINING THE AMERICAN JEWISH
EXPERIENCE IN TERMS OF CITIZENSHIP
With the election of George Washington, the Jewish congregations of the new republic issued a series of congratulatory letters, and the Jewish community of Newport, Rhode Island received a return note from President Washington. It represents one of the most extraordinary statements defining the ideals associated with American society and frames some of this nation's key civic values. The letter serves as an important element in defining and shaping the "Contract" between Jews and America:

> The Citizens of the United States of America have a right to applaud themselves for giving to Mankind examples of an enlarged and liberal policy: a policy worthy of imitation. All possess alike liberty of conscience and immunities of citizenship. It is now no more that toleration is spoken of, as if it was by the indulgence of one class of people that another enjoyed the exercise of their inherent natural rights. For happily the Government of the United States, which gives to bigotry no sanction, to persecution no assistance, requires only that they who live under its protection, should demean [= distinguish] themselves as good citizens. ("To Bigotry No Sanction")

Washington's concluding paragraph perfectly expresses the ideal relationship between the government, its individual citizens and, more pointedly, the Jewish community:

> May the Children of the Stock of Abraham, who dwell in this land, continue to merit and enjoy the good will of the other Inhabitants;

while every one shall sit under his own vine and fig tree, and there shall be none to make him afraid. ("To Bigotry No Sanction")

In the following study, we will attempt to assess in broadest terms the relationship of American Jews with this country—what I would like to characterize as the Jewish Contract with America. While this assessment cannot hope to be comprehensive, we can endeavor to sketch a useful picture of this relationship in its social and political dimensions and therefore come to a better means by which to define this Jewish contract with America—how it has developed and where it is heading. To start, we may note that the very concept of American citizenship can help to provide an effective means through which to grasp this nation's uniqueness and the opportunities readily made available to Jews and others. The distinctions that make American citizenship special have been defined by W. Steger as follows:

> The United States is one of the few countries in the world that does not make citizenship dependent on ancestry, on race, or on membership in a certain religious group. Instead, common principles and values that are enshrined in the country's Constitution bind the citizens of this country—regardless of race, class, or religious creed. . . . Consider the first three words of the Constitution—"We the People." Three seemingly innocuous and yet powerful words, here is the essence of why the United States was exceptional at the time of the Constitution's adoption—the insistence that the authority of government is not derived from God or some higher authority, as was previously thought more or less common, but from the consent of the governed.[1]

This concept of American citizenship demarcates the terms of a liberal, social contract that, by any measure, is exceptional.

## THE UNDERLYING PRINCIPLES OF THE CONTRACT

Contracts only work if there are a shared set of assumptions and beliefs, mutual commitments, and outcomes that benefit and enhance the parties to such an understanding ("What is Society Contract Theory"; Browne; Rusling). From the inception of the United States, American Jewry has identified with the key social norms and political symbols of this society, and Jewish institutions have reflected not only the core terminology of American society but also the structural characteristics of the federal governmental system, itself. The Jewish Contract with America can be understood in the context of how, as a polity, the Jewish community parallels the American political model, with reference to decision-making, geographical distribution, and the separation of powers.

For example, various American Jewish organizations at different points in their evolution, have taken on names with self-consciously symbolic "American" references, including "*United* Jewish Communities," "*American* Jewish *Congress*," "*Union* for Reform Judaism," and "*United* Synagogue of *America* (USA)." The governance and structural functions of American Jewish institutions all reflect two core elements: The use of a federalist system, involving national, regional or state, and local levels of governance; and the existence of separation of powers, consisting of the distribution of assignments and roles among the various governing bodies. The contract can likewise be examined in the context of four core American principles: competition, voluntarism, pluralism, and multiculturalism.

A number of parameters define such a contract. These include the legal framework associated with any contractual arrangement. Yet beyond the formal concepts that might describe and help to frame the relationship, one finds both supporting social values and implied political understandings and/or guarantees. Over the course of time, certain compelling historical experiences lend credence to the notion of a shared story. These events are often joined by celebratory moments that serve as symbolic statements, affirming the deeply held connections that bind these parties together. Finally, one often finds ideological beliefs embodied in national stories that serve to embellish these special connections further. Political scientist Daniel Elazar has offered four principles that describe the special components that can frame the contractual experience for American Jewry. These can be summarized as follows (107–08):

1.  **An Emphasis on Tradition rather than Ideology**: American democracy was not framed around a distinctive set of ideological political beliefs but rather grew organically out of a political tradition comprised of federalism, representative democracy, and communitarian values. American leaders over the course of our nation's history have tended to focus their energies toward advancing cultural and political traditions rather than advancing specific ideological causes. This has been particularly important to Jews who are concerned that special interests or ideological principle might dominate

the political framework of this nation. That this has not been the case has made America more welcoming and engaging to minorities than has proven to be the case elsewhere.

2.  **An Emphasis on Agrarianism as opposed to Urbanism**: The values of individualism, religiosity, and shared responsibility, reflecting America's origins in a rural culture, have been the dominant social values of the early Americans rather than a focus on urban notions of elitism, privilege and property. The early founders, representing America's agrarian roots, thus reflected a leadership style and vision at the time more in sync with Jewish sensibilities.

3.  **An Emphasis on Federalism versus Centralism**: For Elazar the United States represents a society focused on the distribution of power as against its centralization. For Jews, who had lived under authoritarian systems, this concept of separation of powers has been particularly welcoming.

4.  **An Emphasis on Messianism in opposition to Fatalism**: This connotes a society framed around the dreams and possibilities of constructing a different future, where other social systems failed to offer a coherent, transformative vision. A form of American "messianic internationalism" seems to be aligned in many ways with a Jewish prophetic tradition that has biblical foundation. America's focus on remaking the world in the image of democracy is particularly appealing to Jews. Similarly, Jews like to join with other religious communities in articulating a moralistic political perspective for this nation, where religious values over time influence (but do not dictate) public standards.

As Elazar reminds us, few Jews, arriving in this country, and thus becoming a part of this new political experiment, fully understood the elements of the American political process. Initially, they tended to focus on the Presidency, in part based on their prior political encounters, where all power was concentrated around an authoritarian framework of governance.

Secondly, Jews, due to the nature of their religious tradition, have been naturally focused on the supremacy of "Law." If the Torah was the center of gravity for Judaism's legal orientation, then for these new Americans a particular orientation had to be placed on this nation's legal system. As such, Jews have tended to focus their interests on the courts and the rule of law as the basis for their initial encounter with the core values and ideals of Americanism.

For Elazar, core Jewish values of *Kehillah* (community), *Kedoshim* (sacred or holy mission), *Tzedakah* (justice), and *Shalom* (pursuit of peace/happiness) were seen as aligned with American concepts developed in the course of building the nation, in particular, loyalty and sacred duty, civil liberties and rights, and the idea of "life, liberty and the pursuit of happiness." For example, the pluralistic nature of this society is reflected in how American business has come to understand the diversity of this country. This same access and acceptability can also be found within American popular culture: In this respect, Jewish humor has often served as a bridge between mainstream American society and Jewish ideas and values. Americans have come to embrace Jews. Language also reflects this connection: Yiddish terms have become an integral part of the nation's vocabulary. As one of my colleagues suggested when describing the special connection that Jews have with American society, "Americans like us so much that they want to marry our sons and daughters."

## BUILDING A COMMUNITY

A set of historical events have, over time, created the framework defining the special and unique connection that has helped establish the parameters for the Jewish Contract with America. This relationship begins to take form from nearly the beginning of the history of the settlement of America by Europeans, when twenty-three Portuguese Jews arrived in New Amsterdam in 1654 from Recife, Brazil. They requested the right to relocate to the Dutch colony; what followed would be a series of letters between the colony's Governor, Peter Stuyvesant, and members of the Dutch West India Company in Holland. In the end, over the Governor's objections, specific instructions (April 26, 1655) regarding the status of this community were forwarded to the colony:

> Therefore after many deliberations we have finally decided and resolved to apostille upon [= endorse] a certain petition presented by said Portuguese Jews (January 1655) that these people may travel and trade to and in New Netherlands and live and remain there, provided the poor among them shall not become a burden to the company or to the community, but be supported by their own nation. You shall now govern yourself accordingly. ("Looking Back")

Arguably, this is the first articulation of the Jewish Contract with America. Note especially that the last sentence quoted above provides a framework of self-governance for American Jewry that would lead to the creation of a set of interlocking religious, cultural, political, and social service organizations that over the course of 350 years have helped to sustain and to integrate Jews into the fiber of American life and culture.

In September 1728, to take another example, Congregation Shearith Israel of New York formally adopted a set of by-laws, marking the oldest constitution created by a Jewish community in North America, including the following statement:

> If any poor person should happen to come to this place and should want the assistance of the sinagog [= synagogue], the parnaz [= religious leader] is hereby impowered to allow every poor person for his maintenance the sum of eight shillings p'r week, and no more. . . . Those poor of this congregation that shall apply for sedaca [= charity] shall be assisted with as much as the parnaz and his assistants shall think fit [*sic*]. (Marcus, *The Jew in the American World* 59)

## RIGHTS

There are a number of important rights established through the American democratic process that became integral parts of the Jewish Contract with America. Among them are the following:

### Religious Rights and Freedoms

The successful battle for religious freedom in Virginia records a vital chapter in the story of religious liberty in America. James Madison, deeply influenced by the ideas of the Enlightenment, successfully argued that "toleration" should be changed to "free exercise" of religion. For Madison, religious liberty was not a concession by the state or the established church, but an inalienable and natural right of every citizen. Madison played a pivotal role by leading the fight that persuaded the Virginia Legislature to adopt in 1786 Thomas Jefferson's "Bill for the Establishment of Religious Freedom." The first draft of the declaration argued for the "fullest toleration in the exercise of religion according to the dictates of conscience" ("Virginia Act"). In 1791, the free exercise of religion as proclaimed in the Virginia Declaration of Rights became a part of the First

Amendment to the US Constitution, guaranteeing all Americans freedom of conscience:

> Congress shall make no law respecting an establishment of religion, or prohibiting the free exercise thereof; or abridging the freedom of speech, or of the press; or the right of the people peaceably to assemble, and to petition the government for a redress of grievances.

By the time of the ratification of the First Amendment, all of the other Anglican-based state-established religious systems (except that found in Maryland) had been rescinded. The influence of the Congregationalist Church in New England would last longer. Not until 1818 in Connecticut and finally in 1833 in Massachusetts would the state constitutions be amended to complete the national disestablishment of religion. Beyond the symbolic and personal statements of American leadership, the Constitutional principles of American democracy have clearly enabled and shaped Jewish political engagement. The Constitution of the United States confirms the equal legal standing of all Americans, regardless of religion, when the Founding Fathers confirmed Article Six of the Constitution, which contains a further political safeguard—the prohibition of any form of a "religious test" as a qualification to hold public office:

> The Senators and Representatives before mentioned, and the Members of the several State Legislatures, and all executive and judicial Officers, both of the United States and of the several States, shall be bound by Oath or Affirmation, to support this Constitution; but no religious Test shall ever be required as a Qualification to any Office or public Trust under the United States.[2]

Also among the underpinnings basic to this nation's creation was the commitment of its founders to ensuring religious liberty and church-state separation, as expressed in the First Amendment to the Constitution (cited above). Indeed, as early as 1787, with the adoption of the Northwest Ordinance, the religious rights of all were affirmed in a specific contractual framework:

> No person, demeaning [= conducting] himself in a peaceable and orderly manner, shall be molested on account of his mode of worship or religious sentiments. . . . ("Northwest Ordinance")

Jonas Phillips petitioned the Pennsylvania Constitutional Convention, seeking to apply the same rights of political participation and access as afforded

in the federal Constitution to the practices related to the Commonwealth of
Pennsylvania (September 7, 1787):

> To swear and believe that the New Testament was given by divine
> inspiration is absolutely against the religious principle of a Jew, and
> is against his conscience to take any such oath. . . . Therefore if the
> honourable convention shall in their wisdom think fit and alter the
> said oath…then the Israelites will think themselves happy to live un-
> der a government where all religious societys are on equal footing.
> ("General Order No. 11 [1862]")

Despite the legal imperative of equality and political access as called for
within the Constitution, among a number of states the battle for Jewish representation would take considerably longer. Maryland would seat its first Jewish
representative in 1826, with the passage of the so-called "Jew Bill." Earlier,
Jacob Henry of North Carolina would be granted a seat in 1809 following his
eloquent appeal:

> The religion I profess inculcates every duty which man owes to his
> fellow man; it enjoins upon its votaries the practice of every virtue,
> and destination of every vice; it teaches them to hope for the favor
> of heaven exactly in proportion as their lives have been directed by
> just, honorable, and beneficent maxims. . . . At any rate, Mr. Speaker,
> I am sure that you cannot see anything in this religion, to deprive me
> of my seat in this house. (Marcus, *The Jew in the Modern World*, rev.
> ed. 103–04)

## The Right to Organize

Throughout American Jewish history we can observe a series of efforts to unify
the community around specific political concerns, both domestic and international. The first formal effort to organize American Jewry took place with the
establishment of the Central Religious Council in 1841, within whose charter
it is stated:

> It is expected that the Central Religious Council will watch over the
> state of religion, and use every proper occasion to exhort the people
> in sermons or lectures. . . . (Leeser)

Over the decades numerous organizing efforts have been undertaken
to organize groups to act on behalf of the Jewish community. These include
two institutions that were established during the Nineteenth Century: the
Board of Deputies of American Israelites in 1859 and the Union of American

Hebrew Congregations in 1883. In 1906, in response to the Kishenev Pogroms in Poland, the American Jewish Committee was formed and in its "Statement of Purpose" declared:

> We can, however, all unite for the purpose of aiding all Jews who are persecuted, or who are suffering from discrimination in any part of the world on account of their religious beliefs, and we can at the same time, unite for the purpose of ameliorating the condition of our brethren in faith . . . (Marcus 236)

### The Right to Petition

On December 17, 1862 General Ulysses S. Grant issued *General Order Number 11,* restricting Jewish access, trade and movement in parts of the Tennessee River Valley. This order stated in part:

> The Jews as a class violating every regulation of trade established by the Treasury Department, and also Department orders, are hereby expelled from the Department. ("Judaic Treasures")

In response, a letter of petition was forwarded to President Lincoln by representatives of the Jewish community on December 29, 1862, urging the White House to rescind Grant's directive:

> General Order Number 11 issued by General Grant at Oxford, Miss., commands all post commanders to expel Jews without distinction within twenty-four hours from his Department. The undersigned good and loyal citizens of the United States, for many years engaged in legitimate business as merchants, feel greatly insulted and outraged by this inhuman order; the carrying out of which would be the grossest violation of the Constitution and our rights as good citizens under it. . . . We respectfully ask your immediate attention to this enormous outrage on all law and humanity and pray for your effectual and immediate imposition. ("Judaic Treasures")

In response to Jewish protests, the President instructed General-in-Chief, H. W. Halleck of the War Department to issue a directive to General Grant to rescind this order. On January 4, 1863, the following message was conveyed to the General:

> A paper purporting to be General Orders, N. 11, issued by you December 17, has been presented here. By terms it expels all Jews from your department. If such order has been issued, it will be immediately revoked. ("Judaic Treasures")

In December of 1870, at the request of Jewish leaders, President Grant issued a letter of protest to the government of Romania, regarding Benjamin Peixotto, a Jewish-American who had been appointed to the position of US Consul to Romania. This correspondence came in direct reaction to the decision by Romanian authorities to reject Peixotto's credentials because he was a Jew and urged the Romanian government to reinstate the American representative:

> The United States, knowing no distinction of her own citizens on account of religion or nativity, naturally believes in a civilization the world over, which will secure the same universal values. ("American Statesmen on Religion")

Over time, other symbolic statements and defining actions would add to this contractual understanding, including the actions undertaken by Presidents Grover Cleveland[3] and Theodore Roosevelt on behalf of Russian Jewry.[4] Among the most significant actions undertaken by a President, as part of this special connection relating Jewish engagement with America, involved the historic decision by President Harry Truman's to recognize the State of Israel in May of 1948 (Sachar 610–11).

## PRESERVING THEIR STATUS

Jews employed the principle of "equal footing" as part of their nineteenth-century strategy to gain parallel recognition. Following the death of President William Henry Harrison, President John Tyler called for a national day of prayer that was specifically directed to "Christian people." Jacob Ezekiel, a prominent Jewish leader from Richmond, Virginia, sought clarification by writing to the President, seeking his views concerning "those who do not profess Christianity . . ." (Sarna and Dalin 121).

Jews were sensitive to sectarian expressions directed exclusively toward Christians. In 1844 Jews protested South Carolina Governor James H. Hammond's "Thanksgiving Proclamation," denoting that the United States was a "Christian land." In a letter to the Governor, they addressed this concern: "The undersigned, Israelites of Charleston, deem it due to themselves as American freemen, sternly and solemnly to protest against the language and spirit of the Proclamation" ("The Israelites of South Carolina.").

## INTERNAL OPPORTUNITIES, EXTERNAL THREATS

These legal and social concepts are joined by a set of particular policies and defining moments that have helped to shape and direct the Jewish Contract with America. Initially, the tale must be told through the broad lens of images and expectations that were brought by immigrants to America. For Jews, from the outset America was identified as the "Golden Medina" (Brown n.p.), that special and safe place devoid of oppression and religious intolerance. The sense of total security and acceptance within American society, however, would emerge over time. In comparative terms, the American experience, even from the start, was understood to be a far more welcoming environment in comparison to the world of Eastern Europe, the former home of most of those new arrivals.

## DEFINING THEIR IDENTITY

How was American Jewry to understand this unique experiment in democracy and religious liberty? The question of loyalty was introduced during the nineteenth century by Jews, as they struggled with the notion of preserving their Jewish heritage while embracing American culture. For example, note this statement from an 1872 editorial in the *American Israelite*:

> No honest man can or will sacrifice his conviction to any earthly advantage or human institution; if he does, he is no longer a free and responsible moral agent. . . . In all matters touching the peace and prosperity of the society, the administration of justice and the preservation of personal liberty, I am a citizen first, and the duties I owe to my country must be performed first and last. . . . But if I [*sic.*] my government enacts laws or imposes duties contrary to that conviction, I am an Israelite first and would treat my country in a state of rebellion against me. . . . Therefore my God and then my country is as good a motto as any. . . . (Marcus, *The Jew in the Modern World* 206)

## THE IDEA OF ZION WITHIN AMERICAN SOCIETY

The concept of Israel is rooted in the American mindset. nineteenth century Christian Zionism left its mark in framing the centrality of the Holy Land in the religious and social consciousness of America (Safran 15–16). One example would be the efforts to attach biblical names to cities and places within this nation.

Drawing on their loyalty to scripture, prominent American leaders envisioned a Jewish presence being reborn in the Holy Land (Palestine). The biblical links to the Jewish people's vision of statehood and national identity would remain embedded within the evolution of American religious and political thought. This new constitutional regime promised a society secure for Jews, however they might choose to define themselves. ". . . It was a new kind of promised land, at once more seductive and subversive than anything seen since the days of Alexandria" (Lerner 82). The vision of American abundance became intertwined with the vision of America as a haven. Interpreting American life in intensely spiritual terms, Jewish newcomers tended to view their new material existence as an integral part of the New Jerusalem (Heinze 40).

## CONSTRUCTING A NEW AMERICAN JEWISH IDENTITY

It was in the post-Second World War era that the Jewish Contract with America was fundamentally redefined and given both additional dimension and a new and more expansive direction. During this period Jews were able to see themselves no longer as social outsiders or an immigrant class but rather as an integral part of the American experience. In response, Jews needed to address the challenges of becoming part of this society's middle class.

Such transformation was shaped in part by an array of domestic opportunities, including new legislative initiatives, providing Jews and other minorities with the ability to advance their lives and careers. Similarly, the social relocation of Jews from urban centers to suburbia also presented both new challenges and opportunities to identify with the emerging values of the middle class. At the same time, with the birth of the State of Israel, there was a perceived tension between Jewish identity and American loyalty, resulting in a need to define boundaries and demarcate relationships. This dilemma raised concerns for some within the community about how they would be perceived by other Americans. In particular, the fear of renewed anti-Semitism, driven by a concern over the issue of dual-loyalty, was one of the factors in this debate.

Possibly no piece of legislation was more responsible for this social transition than the 1944 "Servicemen's Readjustment Act," more familiarly known as the "GI Bill." It afforded thousands of Jewish veterans, along with their fellow countrymen, the opportunity to participate more fully in the growth of the American middle class through educational opportunities and employment benefits (Diner 260–61). The bill provided for loans and grants that enabled veterans to open businesses, secure a college education or professional training, and made available funding so that young families could purchase homes.

Anthropologist Riv-Ellen Prell offers these thoughts about the engagement of Jews with American culture in this post-war period:

> The important scholarship on suburbs located Jews in a dominant discourse of whiteness, consumption, privilege, and cultural shallows. Suburbs proved to be places that for some period of time transformed and democratized ways of being Jewish. They fostered political activism and solidified racial privilege. They held out hopes for acculturation and assimilation and they dashed some as well. (Diner 48)

For some American Jews, the birth of the State of Israel would raise the question of "dual loyalty." The creation of a Jewish state compelled the American Council for Judaism to issue a statement, defending their position on American patriotism and loyalty: "To Americans of Jewish faith it is a foreign state. Our single and exclusive national identity is to the United States" (Sachar 720).

There are parallel contractual notions within the Jewish communal system involving both domestic (concept of "collective responsibility") and international commitments (i.e., involving the principle of "shared obligations") as defined in the agreement associated with the creation and operation of the Jewish Agency, representing similar agreements that the United States government itself has created in defining its relationship to the states and to international organizations and foreign countries.

In order to clarify issues of Israel-Diaspora relations and to forestall any possibility that the dual-loyalty charge could be raised against American Jews, Jacob Blaustein, President of the American Jewish Committee in 1950, set in motion a series of negotiations with Israeli Prime Minister David Ben Gurion and Foreign Minister Moshe Sharett concerning this question. These conversations lead to a series of letters that have served to define and shape this arrangement. In setting the tone for these discussions, Blaustein stated that:

> We must . . . sound a note of caution to Israel and its leaders. . . . It must recognize that the matter of good will between its citizens and those of other countries is a two-way street—that Israel also has a

> responsibility in this situation . . . of not affecting adversely the sen-
> sibilities of Jews who are citizens of other states by what it says or
> does. . . . American Jews vigorously repudiate any suggestion or im-
> plication that they are living in exile. . . . To American Jews, America
> is home. (Sachar 721)

The promise of Israel, with its repercussions for the status of American Jewry, created, at least for some within the American Jewish community, the challenge of constructing a framework that would serve to define the connection and relationship between the Diaspora and Israel.

## THE RISE OF EXTERNAL THREATS: MCCARTHYISM AND ITS IMPACT

Beyond the internal dimensions of a changing American Jewry in the post-Second World War era, external threats emerged that had profound implications for the American Jewish community and its sense of security. Just as this period offered internal possibilities for Jews, a series of threats loomed beyond the community that might well have undermined and destroyed these possibilities and the possibilities of achieving the "American Dream." Historian Hasia Diner, writing on this theme, suggests that:

> Jewish anxiety about the escalation of anti-Communist rhetoric and
> the spillover from words into deeds also reflected the fact that Jews
> had been over-represented among the supporters of left-wing causes
> in the United States throughout the twentieth century. (Diner 277)

In 1950 Ethel and Julius Rosenberg were found guilty of conspiracy to commit espionage; the charges related to the passing of information about the atomic bomb to the Soviet Union. The two of them were ultimately executed in 1953. This case created a high degree of nervousness among Jews in America. The political witch-hunts conducted by Senator Joseph McCarthy and the activities of the House Committee on Un-American Activities during the early to mid-1950s raised concerns about an increase in anti-Semitism. Jews found themselves walking a tightrope: On the one hand, they found ways to affirm their anti-Communism, while on the other to affirm the tactics of the anti-Communists (Diner 280).

If the 1950s can be perceived as a decade marked by fear and uncertainty for American Jewry, then the repudiation of McCarthyism led the way to the 1960s, which witnessed the emergence of a heightened sense of Jewish political engagement and activism. Jews emerged as key players in the liberal, progressive agenda of the civil rights era and as activists within the Vietnam anti-war movement. With this came new challenges regarding how far Jews could publicly embrace controversial policies without endangering their self-interests and the community's well-being. This period was marked as a time in which Jews were seen to be politically at odds with one another; a reality that reinforced a growing sense of self-assuredness within the Jewish community. At the same time, the 1967 Six-Day War generated a sense of Jewish pride.

The years following the Second World War in part defined the challenges facing American Jewry and proved decisive in shaping their role as a minority community within a larger culture. The new realities of the presence of a Jewish State, along with the heightened visibility of Jews within American society, provided this community with an opportunity to embrace the American experience more fully. Even the divisions within the community over specific domestic and foreign policies were perceived by the Jewish community as testimony to their greater sense of civic assuredness and security (Windmueller).

## CREATING A "CIVIL RELIGION" FOR AMERICAN JEWRY

The political passions of American Jewry have to some extent created what Jonathan Woocher has called the "Civil Religion" of American Jewry: This concept of civil religion has served to further the alignment of Jewish interests and social values with American politics. Over time, there has been a blurring of political behavior and engagement within American Jewish culture. American civil religious rituals, such as a Presidential Inauguration, Thanksgiving, and Memorial Day, serve as vehicles of national, religious self-understanding. Since the earliest days of the nation, American Jews have maintained their own interpretations of American civil religion, which have usually accompanied ideologies of Jewish civil religion.

Some writers, in particular, have focused on the shedding of ethnic otherness in favor of a closer identification with American values, while others have affirmed that the central values of liberty, justice, and freedom stem from God's laws, as seen from a Jewish perspective. Where the saliency of the Jewish political tradition has not encountered a vigorous opposite trend within

American society, stemming from vernacular folk values, the process of secularization, or the natural rights tradition protecting the individual, American Jews have continued to structure their civil religious consensus and organizational life according to Jewish tenets. However, when conflicts have occurred between historical Jewish responses and American values, Jewish civil religion has tended to make accommodation to American societal norms.

Authors such as J. D. Salinger, Norman Mailer, Philip Roth, Saul Bellow, Chaim Potok, Leon Uris, Herman Wouk, Cynthia Ozick and Bernard Malamud, along with more contemporary writers, including Paul Auster, Allegra Goodman, Michael Chabon and Jonathan Safran Foer, have contributed to the conversation about the nature of Jewish identity in America and, in particular, the place of Jewish religious identity in the American story. The alignment of Jewish ideals with American political interests seems particularly appropriate for American Jews. As a result, politics has become a natural extension and expression of Jewish principles and political priorities that are part and parcel to the Jewish Contract with America.

In the aftermath of the Holocaust and with the rebirth of a Jewish State, a new type of symmetry has started to take shape, reflecting American Jewish identity. As Diner notes, "American Jews believed that in some way their fate and that of the Jewish state had been bound together by the Holocaust" (321). Similarly, in the aftermath of the Six-Day War a heightened sense of American Jewish engagement and connectedness with Israel had begun to emerge and ". . . the burst of identification and creativity awakened by the State of Israel itself was energizing virtually every facet of Jewish life in the United States . . ." (Sachar 742). In the years following, Israel has become a central focus within American Jewish life, and in turn, America has become the security framework in which Israel remains viable, insuring that this particular connection is maintained. Philanthropy, political activity, education, religious life, and culture all have been directed toward an Israel-centered ideology.

Jonathan Woocher has captured the interplay between the Holocaust and creation of the Jewish State and the impact both together have had on American Jewish consciousness when he suggested that American Jewry had constructed its own "civil Judaism" (71): ". . . The underlying conviction of the civil religion is that Jewishness and Americanness are mutually reinforcing. A good Jew is a good citizen and a good American—and we have much to bring and much to receive from our involvement in communal welfare" (Fisher 5).

Diner has described the intersection between Judaism and Americanism in this context in the following manner: "Negotiating between American and

Jewish identities, they [Jews] operated with a sense of empowerment. They did not believe that they had to accept America, as it was, nor did they see Judaism as a fixed entity that they could not mold to fit their needs. They could put their impress on both to ease the traumas of accommodation and to bring the two into harmony" (1–2). This capacity to "negotiate" between two identities in many ways allowed the American Jews to emerge successfully within this society as a force that not only influences the nation's culture and politics, but also reshapes Judaism in an American context.

In his memoirs, Arthur Hertzberg (1921–2006), a prominent Conservative rabbi, scholar and social activist, also struggled with two competing themes. The first, was previously raised by Henry Adams, regards the nature of "Americanism," and the second the issues of religious identity and assimilation, was introduced by Alexis de Tocqueville (*Democracy in America*) and raised again later by the Yiddish writer Sholem Aleichem in his novel, *Motl Peyse, the Cantor's Son* (Hertzberg 451–55).[5] In referencing these works, Hertzberg raised the question "what does it mean to be a Jew in the Diaspora?" and, more specifically, "what does it mean to be a Jew in the American context?" This tension can also be seen in different forms of Jewish political expression. As Steven Cohen suggests: "Modernity, then, can be credited with establishing Jewish politics—be it the politics of integration (liberalism) or of group survival (pro-Israelism)—as new forms of group identification" (153).

## JEWISH POLITICAL ADVOCACY

The infrastructure associated with American Jewish advocacy must be recognized to be central to the success of the community in advancing its political interests—especially in terms of its overarching mission to protect the welfare and safety of Jews residing in the United States and/or elsewhere and to advance those causes that contribute to the general enrichment and well being of an American society, in which Jews continue to play a decisive role. The success of the Jewish community in advancing these goals is a result of the successful alignment of the extensive organizational apparatus that remains committed to these core priorities of the community. This involves an extensive commitment by American Jewry to participation in the civic and political culture of this nation, as well as the financial efforts the community has exerted in support of electoral campaigns, political parties, and specific causes.

The core policies of this enterprise have for sixty years shaped and/or re-flected an ideology of social activism, thereby creating a synergy between this community's political identity and the interests and behavior of democratic liberalism. The process of decision-making itself duplicates the federalist mod-el of geographically dispersed centers of authority and action, a local-national configuration of power, and a series of checks and balances.

Competing institutional players and individual elites have sought to ac-cess and shape both Jewish and general public opinion, and, in the process, have further attempted to capture the mantle of "who speaks for the Jews." Jewish political behavior involves two modalities: "consensus-building," the idea of securing a plurality of support in order to articulate a shared vision regarding mutually-agreed upon action, and the principle of "coordinating" functions, so as to maximize the use of communal resources.

Jews have played four distinctive roles in developing their contract with America over the course of their American political engagement. Initially, as noted above, they served as *"Petitioners,"* requesting actions to be taken on their behalf; this political framework was most evident between 1654 and 1870. The second political role involved individual Jews who created personal relationships with key elites and who acted on behalf of the community by promoting or advancing its interests. This *"Personality"* phase of Jewish ac-tivism covered a sixty-year period from 1870–1930. The third construct of collective engagement, created a *"Participant"* role model of Jewish political behavior. This pattern became dominant between 1930 and 1960. The final political stage of Jewish engagement can be identified as the *"Partner"* stage, where Jews have been seen as power-players within the American political sys-tem. Commencing with the mid- to late 1960s, this mode of activism has been dominant over the last fifty years.

In considering more closely how Jews over the course of the past hun-dred years have expressed their political passions, one can further identify six basic time-segments that can serve to define the community's engagement with the world of public policy and social activism:

- *The Politics of Security (1906–38):* As the community began to evolve and stabilize, the process of Americanization witnessed a period of defensive responses, designed to offset nativism and anti-Semitism. The term "civic protective program" was employed by community leaders to define the work necessary to ensure Jewish security.
- *The Politics of War and Death (1939–45):* In this period there were

two themes that at times competed: the goal of creating a Jewish State and thus fulfilling the Zionist vision, and a preoccupation with the issues of the Second World War and the refugees it produced. During this era, the field of Jewish community relations labeled their political responsibilities as "Jewish public relations."

- *Politics of Accommodation (1948–67):* The civil rights revolution not only changed the political playing field for African-Americans but also altered the political power structure for all citizens, especially American Jews, who took a lead in embracing civil rights issues along side the black community.

- *Politics of Self-Interest (1967–80):* This era was defined by the startling events surrounding the Six-Day War and the reclamation of Soviet Jewry. Correspondingly, the American Jewish community became infused with a new sense of its own identity and political assertiveness. Some have suggested that this heightened sense of Jewish political activism that defined this era could be labeled the "civil religion of American Jewry" (a point already discussed above), thereby reflecting the deep sense of engagement Jews had with the political process.

- *The New Internal Challenges (1981–2001):* This period has been dominated by the emergence of new challenges and threats, as well as the changing character of Jewish political advocacy. At the outset, the "Peace for Galilee Campaign" (Israel's invasion of Lebanon in 1981) and the first Palestinian Intifada (1987–91) created significant debate and dissent emerging both within and outside of the American Jewish community. During this period the community has seen the growth of single-issue constituencies involving both international and domestic concerns, and with the onset of the Oslo Peace Process, there appears to be a changing level of interest in advocacy associated with Israel and other core issues.

- *The Challenges from Without (2001–):* Since the events of September 11th, new sets of challenges face Jews, not only at home but also internationally, in light of the rise of global terrorism. American Jews focus themselves politically through two competing lenses: a broader liberal ideology that frames Jewish and, by extension, universal values, and a narrower, more sharply defined political engagement through interest-group politics, specifically defending and embracing Jewish self-interests. In contemporary times, several competing ideas remain in play, refracted by these different elements of Jewish experience and practice.

Adam Dickter offered a number of cogent political idioms that give definition to the American Jewish orientation:

> **Nationalist Orientation vs. Accommodational Behavior:** Historically, Jews operated in one of two political spheres, either understanding their political destiny as tied to a national (i.e., Jewish) perspective, seeking to create a Jewish state or to work toward sustaining it, or striving for some type of acceptance by making political compromises whereby they would accommodate to the social environment around them. In other terms, we might describe these characteristics, as "going it alone" vs. "fitting in."
>
> **Judaism as Americanism**: Over the course of the twentieth century a body of political thought would emerge that would define Jews as full partners in the American story and where "Judeo-Christian values" would frame the social fabric of this nation. This "melting pot" concept would allow Jews full access into the mainstream of the society.
>
> **"Be a Jew on the Street and an American at Home"**: Historian David Biale has suggested that unlike the mindset of the Enlightenment where Jews publicly shed their Jewishness, the American context represents precisely the reverse idea, where one can reject the melting pot viewpoint in favor of a Jewish political assertion.
>
> **Never Forget:** "The commanding voice of Auschwitz" would not allow a Jew to forget his/her historical and political distinctiveness. One may understand this concept best when viewing it in the following terms: "failure to support Israel represents a denial of the lessons of the Holocaust."

In each principle area of ideology, geography, leadership competition, styles of decision-making, and the concept of consensus, the Jewish Contract with America has taken on the attributes and behavior of a distinctive subculture of the American polity.

"Lobbying is effective when it is accompanied by the capacity to deliver a substantial number of votes in key elections, when it is able to show that following recommended policies will have desirable human and policy outcomes, and when it is accompanied by past or potential campaign funding. Through PACs and individual giving, and through very effective efforts to get out the Jewish vote, Jews have wielded several of these methods ethically and effectively" (Teutsch). Beyond the support of this informal system of political engagement, the pro-Israel agenda is specifically enhanced by the presence of a formal lobbying process as represented by the "American Israel Public Affairs Committee" (AIPAC) and more recently by "J Street," representing the voice of the Jewish political left as related to Israeli security and the peace process. As Mitchell Bard notes:

> AIPAC was not the first domestic lobby to concern itself with foreign affairs, but it is regarded as the most powerful. In 1998 and 1999, for example, *Fortune Magazine* named AIPAC the second most powerful lobby in Washington after the American Association for Retired Persons (AARP). The lobby strives to remain nonpartisan and thereby keeps friends in both parties. By framing the issues in terms of the national interest, AIPAC can attract broader support than would ever be possible if it was perceived to represent only the interests of Israel. This does not mean AIPAC does not have a close relationship with Israeli officials, it does, albeit unofficially.

He further notes:

> Overall, the Israeli lobby is effective because it enjoys advantages in every area considered relevant to interest group influence. It has (a) a large and vocal membership; (b) members who enjoy high status and legitimacy; (c) a high degree of electoral participation (voting and financing); (d) effective leadership; (e) a high degree of access to decision makers; and (f) public support. Moreover, for reasons at least partly attributable to the lobby's efforts, the lobby's primary objective—a U.S. commitment to Israel—has been accepted as a national interest.

Bard assesses the pro-Israel community's impact:

> In a more rigorous study of 782 policy decisions made from 1945 to 1984, I found the Israeli lobby won; that is, achieved its policy objective, 60 percent of the time. The most important variable was the president's position. When the president supported the lobby, it won 95 percent of the time. At first glance it appears the lobby was only successful because its objectives coincided with those of the president, but the lobby's influence was demonstrated by the fact that it still won 27 percent of the cases when the president opposed its position.
>
> One of the most surprising results, particularly in light of conventional wisdom and evidence presented in case studies, was that the president's position was not significantly affected by the electoral

cycle. Although candidates may appear to pander to Jewish voters, the data indicate the electoral cycle does not affect influence success.

Lobby success also varied depending on the policy at issue. The lobby was very successful in overcoming presidential opposition on economic issues but rarely able to defeat the president on security and political issues. The lobby was more successful on economic issues because most of those were decided in Congress where pro-Israel congressman frequently fought for increased aid levels for Israel, earmarked funds for Israel and adopted amendments to aid bills that were endorsed by the Israeli lobby.

The lobby's lack of success on political issues was most likely a result of the fact that most of these cases were decided in the executive branch where lobby influence is relatively weak. The outcome might also be explained by the tradition of congressional deference to the president on matters of security and diplomacy.

Minority communities often feel as though they have few options in advancing their political agenda, since they perceive that their political clout is concentrated around a defined area of influence. In the case of the Jewish community, this is reflected in its advocacy-work for the State of Israel and in advancing the welfare of Jewish communities worldwide. As long as there is no direct challenge to their credibility or political interests, minority groups can advance their respective agenda. Defined as the "rule of marginal effect" (Isaacs 241), this principle would suggest that interest groups can operate in a sphere of influence as long as their actions do not conflict with the overriding priorities of American foreign policy. It is significant when a minority community can move its primary priorities to be seen as central to the collective interests of the governing elites. The alignment of Jewish concerns for Israel's security and national viability are seen today as integral to American policy priorities.

An interesting example of the limits of Jewish influence can be found in the period of the early nineteenth century, with regard to United States policy toward Russia. In light of Czarist anti-Semitic policies directed against millions of Russian Jews, American Jewish leaders pressed the American government to abrogate the 1832 Commercial Treaty, which had given Russia special trade advantages. United States officials, however, were desirous of maintaining a balance of power with the Far East as a way to offset the Japanese victory over the Russians in 1904–05 (Russo-Japanese War). "The attempt by Jewish leaders to weaken Russia, first by extending financial support to Japan during the war, and then by threatening the market for Russian goods in America, was not in consonance with larger American policy objectives" (Feingold 198).

## INSIGHTS ON ANTI-SEMITISM

In the end, the absence of any experience within American society of state-supported or sponsored anti-Semitism must be seen as particularly significant in framing the case for the uniqueness of the Jewish Contract with America. Possibly no other factor more distinctively defines and sustains the special relationship that Jews have with the United States. With reference to the anti-Semitism, Jerome Chanes, who comments on Jewish public policy matters, has noted the following:

> America is different. A review of anti-Semitism in the United States must take place in the singular context of democratic pluralism, associationalism, and American exceptionalism. What makes America "different" are those constitutional protections, particularly those in the Bill of Rights and the separation of church and state that inform a society of democratic pluralism. It is the rich soil of pluralism that has been inhospitable for the nightshade of anti-Semitism to take firm root, whatever manifestations of anti-Semitism there have been and continue to be. (127)

Polling data on American attitudes toward Israel have reaffirmed over time the "special relationship" that exists between the US and the State of Israel. In many ways, there may be no better indicator of the security and well-being enjoyed by American Jewry than the level of public opinion in support of Israel.

Though similar to the highly favorable attitudes toward Israel in 2005 and 2006, the 71% of Americans viewing Israel favorably today is eight points higher than the 63% recorded last year, and is the highest favorable score for Israel since the 79% recorded during the 1991 Gulf War (Saad). Possibly no other definitive standards can as effectively be employed to determine a society's level of connection and openness to its Jewish population as the presence/absence of anti-Semitism and support for the State of Israel. Employing both standards of assessment, this nation must be seen as unique in its welcoming of Jews and through its support of Israel.

## DEFINING THE DIMENSIONS OF AN AMERICAN JEWISH ECONOMY

The *American Jewish economy* manifests a number of core elements that contribute to its vitality and reflects its deeply embedded connections with core American principles. All these elements are integral to the Jewish Contract with America and therefore deserve careful consideration. The values of competition and choice are essential components of this system. A commitment to the role of *voluntarism* represents another significant feature in expanding its impact and presence. The focus on *innovation and entrepreneurship* emulates the general economic culture. Finally, the commitment to *marketing and consumerism* drives significant elements of the Jewish economic story. Yet, beyond its affinity with these economic principles, there are distinctive Jewish values and an overlay of its communal historical experience that give special purpose and definition to this system, aligning it with the global Jewish enterprise.

The Jewish economy seeks to support three core market principles:

1.   Sustaining Judaism and the Jewish people
2.   Building support for the State of Israel and the Upholding of the Zionist vision
3.   Engaging in Tikkun Olam, the Act of Repairing the World

There are a number of specific elements that define this economic system, each of which is described in some detail below:

1.   Infrastructure
2.   Financial Viability
3.   Global Economy
4.   Communications and Branding
5.   Investments
6.   Leadership

### Infrastructure

Since the late nineteenth century, the Jewish community has invested in hospitals, universities and seminaries, museums, schools, synagogues, camps, JCCs, cemeteries, and agency facilities. In addition, the community manages an extensive amount of property donated and/or operated under the aegis of Jewish organizations. Within this economy, thousands of individuals are employed who perform hundreds of different roles and services, not only contributing to the support and maintenance of the communal system, but also providing an infusion of monies that go back into the larger society. The services provided not only meet the educational, cultural, and religious needs of constituencies within the Jewish community, but further offer assistance and support to thousands of Americans through its social service networks, medical and recreational facilities, thereby relieving the public service sector of having to deliver these programs.

Economists often speak of the *ripple effect,* occurring as a result of a particular economic policy or activity; no doubt the Jewish communal system, as a result of its size and scope of activities, is able to generate services, offer employment, stimulate giving and promote affiliation and engagement. The growing presence of non-Jews as investors, donors, and purchasers of service represents an important undervalued resource. Of particular significance, business and commercial groups from all sectors of the economy are partnering today with the Jewish community to advance various projects and causes, frequently supporting or underwriting particular services or activities of the community.

**Financial Viability**

While there is a body of literature on the overall economic history of the Jewish people, limited attention has been given to the American Jewish economic story.[6] For more than one hundred years, until it ceased publication in 2008, the *American Jewish Year Book* annually provided some comprehensive data on Jewish communal finances.

More recently, Mark Pearlman, writing in *Jinsider* in 2009, suggested that the *Gross Domestic Product* of the Jewish community amounted to $9.7 billion. In his research Pearlman analyzed the different categories of activity and funding over the course of a given fiscal year, in effect to create a Jewish GDP that could measure all of the services and goods produced by the *Jewish economy* within the United States. The Pearlman report noted that the "Jewish GDP study focused on the basic economics of the Jewish community, specifically the distribution and balance of funds throughout Jewish non profit organizations." Among the primary economic elements are these percentages:

1.   Social Welfare: 36%
2.   Education: 32%.
3.   Communal Life: 17%
4.   Advocacy: 4%

5.    Arts: 2%
6.    Arab-Israel: 1%

According to Pearlman, "More than 25 percent of all funds come through the Jewish federation system." Thirty percent of all revenue based on this study was concentrated among the top ten Jewish nonprofits, including UJA/Federation of New York, the Jewish Agency, JDC, Hadassah, and Yeshiva University. In more recent times a sizeable *private Jewish sector* has emerged, consisting of businesses, consulting groups, service providers and professional resources that in some instances compete with the nonprofit sector, while also meeting specialized needs and individualized tastes. This aspect of the Jewish economy has yet to be fully appreciated and correspondingly, its impact has yet to be measured in shaping not only a domestic but global system of resources.

**Global Jewish Engagement: Building an International System**
The international aspects of the American Jewish economy are particularly significant in light of the Diaspora-Israel partnership. Here, one finds not only Jewish philanthropic dollars being provided to Israel and Jewish communities across the world, but also the investment by Jews and others in building infrastructure in Israel and elsewhere.

Federations have collectively raised more than $25 billion since 1948 as part of their annual campaigns, of which over $12 billion or approximately 47% has been earmarked for international concerns, including the Jewish Agency and the American Jewish Joint Distribution Committee. These numbers do not reflect Israel Emergency Campaigns and other special international appeals (*Jewish Federations of North America*).

Correspondingly, institutions such as Hadassah generate significant annual revenues (in 2010 some $44 million) for their on-going programs within Israel, not including specific earmarked projects. In addition to the Jewish National Fund (JNF) which reported revenues in 2010 for their infrastructural programs in Israel of $37 million, there are some thirty "American Friends" organizations that have over the course of the past half-century raised significant resources for the State of Israel and more directly, its universities, social service networks, religious movements, and cultural institutions. These transnational financial institutional partnerships represent collectively one of the largest global non-profit enterprises ever constructed.

Since its inception the State of Israel Bonds Corporation has invested more than $34 billion in the Jewish State, involving approximately a billion dollars a year in additional purchases (*Israel Bonds*).

## Communications and Branding

The community has not only created over time a mature economic system with all of the core components committed to sustaining Jewish life but also has constructed a communications network that today encompasses the internet with its hundreds of Jewish websites and resources, while maintaining its Anglo-Jewish press and publishing houses. The presence of newspapers, books, pamphlets, films, television specials, videos, and CDs adds a distinctive element to the branding of Jewish messages and to the articulation of a set of core values. No economy can operate without the capacity to deliver messages as well as garner input from its consumer base.

## Investments

Every economy must focus on *building equity and ensuring continuity*. One of the core features of the American Jewish economy involves the significant commitment by Jews to invest in their future. This can best be measured by the growth of endowment funds, the establishment of foundations, and the expansion of long-term giving programs.

In 2009 federations reported on community endowment portfolios where holdings were posted in excess of $13 billion. Similarly, the Jewish Funders Network noted: "As the number of Jewish foundations and individual funders has grown—more than doubling in total assets over the past seven years to approximately $30 billion in the United States alone—so has the need for a dynamic international network of philanthropic leaders." As a capital-driven system, the financial health of the community represents the core measure of its ability to market its ideas and messages and promote its services, while reaffirming its brand.

## Leadership

An essential strength of this system has been its ability to develop a strong cadre of lay and professional leaders. This social network has adhered to a set of specific characteristics, including the presence of interlocking directorates whose organizations both share lay leaders and benefit from cross-institutional access and connections. There is high premium placed on leadership recruitment at both the lay and professional levels that has permitted this system to identify, prepare and promote high-quality and engaged individuals. A set of shared leadership characteristics within the professional sector reflects a high degree of specialized training and education, access to professional and institutional networks, and a strong commitment to core institutional and communal outcomes.

## SOME REFLECTIONS ON ECONOMIC FACTORS AND JEWISH POWER

Jews have gained a degree of political credibility due in part to their economic position, not only within the United States, but beyond. The elements introduced here both reflect on the uniqueness of their American experience and their on-going engagement with their global connections and interests. The historical model of interlocking Diaspora communities is in some measure maintained and strengthened within the contemporary world of economic opportunity and growth.

The collective Jewish story in itself becomes a form of credibility. Jews were considered the "other" by both the political elites and masses for centuries by the European elites, operating outside of the established norms and culture of many of these feudal states. In the case of the Jewish people and their universal quest for acceptance, their endurance and adaptability has served to give them credence and eventual recognition. In addition, political interest groups require access and resources in order to deliver on their policy priorities.

## CONCLUSION

The Jewish Contract with America must be viewed within the frame of this country's commitment to cultural diversity and religious pluralism. In order to sustain these ideals, the United States has established a legal framework, which embodies these values. Over the course of some 350 years of a Jewish presence on the North American continent, Jews have embraced this national opportunity to construct a different type of contractual agreement than that which had existed in other Diaspora settings. In the process of the growing American Jewish experience, Jews have become an essential and highly visible element within the structure and culture of this society. As part of this emerging experience, Jews have also had occasion to build new forms of religious expression and create a different type of communal system. The creation of competitive, voluntary models of community has been one of the key contributions made by the Jews of America to the contemporary Jewish scene.

The contract that has emerged between America's Jews and the broader social order of this country encompasses today a number of specific elements, including these ten principles:

1. Religious freedom as central to the Jewish experience and significant to other religious communities in the United States;
2. The separation of church and state as a core ingredient to the success of the American experiment;
3. Israel as a strategic partner to the United States and the maintenance of the unique relationship between Jerusalem and Washington;
4. An educated and engaged American polity, as being critical to this democracy;
5. The nurturing of inter-group cooperation and multicultural engagement as a demonstration of the principles of democracy and coalitional politics;
6. A commitment on the part of this nation to insuring economic and social justice and the fullest inclusion of all citizens within the American experience;
7. The availability to all citizens of basic human and social services, whether offered through governmental resources, the private provider, or the non-profit sector;
8. A commitment on the part of this nation to opposing those forces engaged in terrorism or activities that promote racism, sexism, and anti-Semitism;
9. A commitment to environmental and ecological policies that can and will enhance the health of the global community and the well-being of our planet;
10. International human rights as an extension of the American principles of freedom.

In defining the future of the American Jewish experience, Steven Bayme suggests that a major challenge faces this community in preserving its identity:

> American Jewry, in short, confronts significant challenges, not to
> its status as Jews in America, but rather to its identity as American
> Jews. . . . Whether American Jews envision their future as empow-
> ered and enriched by Judaic heritage or as overwhelmed and demor-
> alized by the reality of assimilation will, in many ways, determine the
> course of future Diaspora history. (161)[7]

Living in this type of cultural setting reminds Jews of the choices and
dilemmas that, at times, they must face. This in turn results in its own creative
energy, allowing minorities the opportunity to flourish, as they both contribute to the larger American culture and negotiate their own ethnic or religious
pathways to preserving their respective heritage and traditions.

Just as historian David Biale has noted the doctrine of Jewish "chosen-
ness," we would see a similar concept employed in defining the idea of America,
as a "chosen" society. The push toward redefining the ethnic arrangements and
cultural connections that have bound groups to the American story, leads to
the introduction of several different models of group engagement. One as introduced by Will Herberg, the "Doctrine of Ethnic Pluralism," allows groups
to preserve and even celebrate their distinctiveness, whereas Horace Kallen's
idea of the "Melting Pot Theory" calls for ethnic integration as the methodology necessary for creating the "ideal American citizen." In more recent times,
Sylvia Barack Fishman has offered us another framework by which we may understand how Jews could redefine the tensions between their ethnic-religious
positions and their American identity.

The success of the American Jewish experiment can be found through
this tension manifest in the Jewish Contract with America, as Jews are con-
stantly negotiating between their "Jewish" and "American" identities. This
battle of identity represents the American story, not only for Jews, but for all
ethnic communities that are a part of this American nation.

## Notes

1. Professor Dr. Werner Steger, Dutchess County Community College. Keynote Address at Naturalization Ceremony. 14 April 2005. Accessed at <http://www.sunydutchess.edu/news/nc1.html>. This site appears no longer to be functional.

2. See, for example, "Constitution of the United States."

3. President Cleveland noted in his 1895 State of the Union Address, ". . . the practice of Russian consuls within the jurisdiction of the United States to interrogate citizens as to their race and religious faith, and upon ascertainment thereof to deny to Jews authentication of passports or legal documents for use in Russia. Inasmuch as such a proceeding imposes a disability which in the case of succession to property in Russia may be found to infringe the treaty rights of our citizens, and which is an obnoxious invasion of our territorial jurisdiction, it has elicited fitting remonstrance, the result of which, it is hoped, will remove the cause of complaint. The pending claims of sealing vessels of the United States seized in Russian waters remain unadjusted. Our recent convention with Russia establishing a modus vivendi as to imperial jurisdiction in such cases has prevented further difficulty of this nature." See "Grover Cleveland: State of the Union Address, 1895."

4. President Theodore Roosevelt issued a letter to Czar Nicholas II, protesting the 1905 Kishinev Pogrom; see "Teddy Roosevelt, Jewish Avenger (1899)."

5. For Sholom Aleichem, see, e.g., *Tevye the Dairyman and Motl the Cantor's Son.*

6. Chiswick and Chiswick; Chiswick and Wenz; B. R. Chiswick, "American Jewry: An Economic Perspective and Research Agenda"; "Economic Status of American Jews"; "The Skills and Economic Status of American Jewry: Trends Over the Last Half Century"; "The Post-War Economy of American Jews"; and a significant body of work from B. R. Chiswick: see <http://tigger.uic.edu/~brchis/jewish.pdf>.

7. See more at Windmueller.

## *Works Cited*

Adams, Henry. *The Education of Henry Adams: An Autobiography*. New York: Penguin, 1995.

Aleichem, Sholom. *Motl Peyse, the Cantor's Son* [Motl Peyse Dem Khazns]. Jerusalem: Hebrew Univ. Magnes, 1997 (Yiddish Edition).

————. *Tevye the Dairyman and Motl the Cantor's Son*. Trans. A. Shevrin. New York: Penguin, 2009.

"American Statesmen on Religion." *Angelfire*. 21 Sept. 2013 <http://www.angelfire.com/journal2/serpentandlion/americanstatesmen.html>.

Bard, Mitchell. "The Israeli and Arab Lobbies." *Jewish Virtual Library*. July 2012. 24 Sept. 2013 <http://www.jewishvirtuallibrary.org/jsource/US-Israel/lobby.html>.

Bayme, Steven. "Jewish Organizational Response to Intermarriage." *Jews in America: A Contemporary Reader*. Ed. Roberta Rosenberg Farber and Chaim Isaac Waxman. Hanover, NH: Brandeis Univ., 1999. 151–62.

Brown, Julia. *Ethnicity and the American Short Story*. New York: Garland, 1997.

Browne, Kevin J. "Introduction to the Social Contract Theory." *Helium.com*. 28 May 2008. 9 Oct. 2013 <http://www.helium.com/items/1059025-introduction-to-the-social-contract-theory>.

Chanes, Jerome. "Anti-Semitism and Jewish Security in Contemporary America: Why Can't Jews Take Yes for an Answer?" *Jews in America: A Contemporary Reader*. Ed. Roberta Rosenberg Farber and Chaim Isaac Waxman. Hanover, NH: Brandeis Univ., 1999. 124–50.

Chiswick, Barry R. "American Jewry: An Economic Perspective and Research Agenda." *Contemporary Jewry* 23 (2002): 156–82; revised and updated in Carmel U. Chiswick, Tikva Lecker and Nava Kahana, eds. *Jewish Society and Culture: An Economic Perspective*. Ramat Gan: Bar-Ilan Univ., 2007. 177–206.

————. "Economic Status of American Jews." *American Jewry: Portrait and Prognosis*. Ed. David M. Gordis and Dorit P. Gary. New York: Behrman, 1997. 247–60; presented at Conference on Policy Implications of the 1990 National Jewish Population Survey, July 1991. Univ. of Judaism, Los Angeles. Revised 1994.

————. "The Post-War Economy of American Jews." *America since the Second World War*. Ed. Peter Y. Medding. Studies in Contemporary Jewry 8. Oxford: Oxford Univ., 1992. 85–101.

————. "The Skills and Economic Status of American Jewry: Trends over the Last Half Century." *Journal of Labor Economics—Special Issue in Honor of Jacob Mincer* 11.1 (January 1993): 229–42; expanded version in Robert S. Wistrich, ed. *Terms of Survival: The Jewish World Since 1945*. London: Routledge, 1995. 115–29.

Chiswick, Barry R. and Carmel U. Chiswick. "Economic Transformation of American Jewry." Vol. 4 of *Encyclopedia of Jewish Culture*. Ed. Yirmiyahu Yovel. Jerusalem: Keter, 2007. 101–06. (Hebrew)

Chiswick, Barry R. and Michael Wenz. "The Linguistic and Economic Adjustment of Soviet Jewish Immigrants in the United States: 1980 to 2000." *Research in Labor Economics* 24 (2006): 179–216.

Cohen, Steven M. *American Modernity and Jewish Identity.* New York: Tavistock, 1983.

"Constitution of the United States." *The Charters of Freedom.* 21 Sept. 2013 <http://www.archives.gov/exhibits/charters/constitution_transcript.html>.

Dickter, Adam. "Rules of Jewish Political Engagement." *The Jewish Week.* 7 Sept. 2012. 24 Sept. 2013 <http://www.thejewishweek.com:8080/blogs/political-insider/rules-jewish-political-engagement>.

Diner, H. R. *The Jews of the United States, 1654 to 2000.* Berkeley and Los Angeles: Univ. of California, 2004.

Elazar, Daniel J. "The Political Tradition of the American Jew." *Traditions of the American Jew.* Ed. Stanley M. Wagner. New York: Ktav, 1977.

Feingold, Henry. *A Midrash on American Jewish History.* Albany: SUNY, 1982.

Fisher, Max. "The Role of an American Jewish Leader in Today's World." *General Assembly Papers.* New York: Council of Jewish Federations and Welfare Funds, 1967.

Fishman, Sylvia Barack. *Negotiating Both Sides of the Hyphen: Coalescence, Compartmentalization and American Jewish Values.* Monograph, Lichter Lecture Series. Cincinnati: Univ. of Cincinnati, 1996.

"General Order No. 11 (1862)." *Wikipedia.* 6 Sept. 2013. 21 Sept. 2013 <http://www.wikipedia.org/wiki/General_Order_No._11_(1862)>.

"Grover Cleveland: State of the Union Address, 1895." *USA Presidents.* 29 Sept. 2013 <http://www.usa-presidents.info/union/cleveland-7.html>.

*Hadassah.* The Women's Zionist Organization of America, Inc. 28 Sept. 2013 <http://www.hadassah.org/site/pp.aspx?c=keJNIWOvElH&b=5571065>.

Heinze, Andrew R. *Adapting to Abundance: Jewish Immigrants, Mass Consumption, and the Search for American Identity.* New York: Columbia Univ., 1990.

Herberg, Will. *Protestant—Catholic—Jew: An Essay in American Religious Sociology.* Chicago: Univ. of Chicago, 1983. (Originally pub. 1960.)

Hertzberg, Arthur. *A Jew in America: My Life and a People's Struggle for Identity.* San Francisco: Harper Collins, 2003.

Isaacs, Stephen D. *Jews and American Politics.* New York: Doubleday, 1974.

*Israel Bonds.* Development Corporation for Israel. 28 Sept. 2013 <http://www.israel-bonds.com/home.aspx>.

"The Israelites of South Carolina." *The Occident and American Jewish Advocate* 2.10 (January 1845). *Jewish-History.com.* Jewish-American History Foundation. 21 Sept. 2013 <http://www.jewish-history.com/occident/volume2/jan1845/churchstate.html>.

*The Jewish Federations of North America.* 28 Sept. 2013 <http://www.jewishfederations.org/>.

*Jewish Funders Network.* 28 Sept. 2013 <http://www.jfunders.org/>.

*Jewish National Fund.* 28 Sept. 2013 <http://www.jnf.org/>.

"Judaic Treasures of the Library of Congress: Order No. 11." *Jewish Virtual Library.* 29 Sept. 2013 <http://www.jewishvirtuallibrary.org/jsource/loc/abe2.html>.

Kallen, Horace M. "Democracy versus the Melting-Pot: A Study of American Nationality." *The Nation* (25 Feb. 1915). *Pluralism and Unity.* Ed. David Bailey, David Halsted. H-Net, Humanities and Social Sciences Online and Michigan State University. 28 Sept. 2013 <http://www.expo98.msu.edu/people/kallen.htm>.

Leeser, Isaac. "Union for the Sake of Judaism." *The Occident and American Jewish Advocate* 3.5 (August 1845). *Jewish-History.com.* Jewish-American History Foundation. 21 Sept. 2013 <http://www.jewish-history.com/occident/volume3/aug1845/union2.html>.

Lerner, Ralph. "Believers and the Founders' Constitution." *Jews and the American Public Square: Debating Religion and Republic.* Ed. Alan Mittleman, Robert Licht, and Jonathan D. Sarna. New York: Rowman and Littlefield, 2002. 71–85.

"Looking Back: Stuyvesant's Failed Efforts to Prohibit Jewish Immigration." *Fight Hatred: Jabotinsky International Center.* 26 April 2010. 21 Sept. 2013 <http://www.fighthatred.com/historical-events/anti-semitic-incidents/688-looking-back-stuyvesants-failed-efforts-to-prohibit-jewish-immigration>.

Marcus, Jacob Rader, ed. *The Jew in the American World: A Source Book.* Detroit: Wayne State Univ., 1996.

———. *The Jew in the Modern World.* Detroit: Wayne State Univ., 1996.

———. *The Jew in the Modern World.* Rev. ed. Cincinnati: Hebrew Union College, 1999.

"Northwest Ordinance." *West's Encyclopedia of American Law.* 2005. *Encyclopedia.com.* 21 Sept. 13 <http://www.encyclopedia.com/topic/Northwest_Ordinance.aspx>.

Pearlman, Mark. "Jewish GDP Study." Jinsider. March 2009. 28 Sept. 2013 <http://www.jinsider.com/gdp>.

Rusling, Louise. "Introduction to the Social Contract Theory." *Helium.com.* 21 July 2007. 9 Oct. 2013 <http://www.helium.com/items/473610-introduction-to-the-social-contract-theory>.

Saad, Lydia. "China Down, France Up in Americans' Ratings: Favorability of Israel Highest Since 1991 Gulf War." *Gallup.* 3 March 2008. 24 Sept. 2013 <http://www.gallup.com/poll/104719/China-Down-France-Americans-Ratings.aspx>.

Sachar, Howard M. *A History of the Jews in America.* New York: Vintage, 1992.

Safran, Nadav. *The United States and Israel.* Cambridge, MA: Harvard Univ., 1963.

Sarna, Jonathan D. and David G. Dalin. *Religion and State in the American Jewish Experience.* Notre Dame: Univ. of Notre Dame, 1997.

"Teddy Roosevelt, Jewish Avenger (1899)." *Jewish Virtual Library.* 29 Sept. 2013 <http://www.jewishvirtuallibrary.org/jsource/US-Israel/TeddyRoosevelt.html>.

Teutsch, David. "Influencing America: Jewish Political Influence." *Sh'ma: A Journal of Jewish Ideas*. 1 Oct. 2004. 24 Sept. 2013 <http://www.shma.com/2004/10/influenc-ing-america-jewish-political-influence/>.

"'To Bigotry No Sanction, to Persecution No Assistance'. George Washington's Letter to the Jews of Newport, Rhode Island, 1790." *Jewish Virtual Library*. 29 Sept. 2013 <http://www.jewishvirtuallibrary.org/jsource/US-Israel/bigotry.html>.

Tocqueville, Alexis de. *Democracy in America: A New Translation*. Trans. Arthur Goldhammer. Google eBook, 2012.

"The Virginia Act for Establishing Religious Freedom." *Religious Freedom Page*. 21 Sept. 2013 <http://religiousfreedom.lib.virginia.edu/sacred/vaact.html>.

"What is Society Contract Theory." *Wiki.Answers.com*. 2013. 21 Sept. 2013 <http://wiki. answers.com/Q/What_is_social_contract_theory>.

Windmueller, Steven. "Jews in the Psyche of America." *Jewish Political Studies Review* 21 (2009). *Jerusalem Center for Public Affairs*. 28 Oct. 2009. 23 Sept. 2013 <http://jcpa. org/article/jews-in-the-psyche-of-america/#sthash.tnbWARjt.dpuf>.

Woocher, Jonathan. *Sacred Survival: The Civil Religion of American Jews*. Bloomington: Indiana Univ., 1986.

# Geography, Demography, and the Jewish Vote

*Ira M. Sheskin*

Data on the number of American Jews is not available from the US Census. This is due to restrictions caused by the separation of church and state and the treatment of Jews by the US Census Bureau as a religious group, rather than as the ethnic group that they also constitute. As a result, the organized American Jewish community has collected its own data via national and local telephone surveys on the demography, geography, and religiosity of American Jews (see *Berman Jewish Databank*).

Various estimates of the number of American Jews are available, ranging from about 5.4 million to about 6.8 million (Sheskin and Dashefsky, "Jewish Population in the United States, 2013"; DellaPergola, "Was it the Demography"; "World Jewish Population, 2013"; Kotler-Berkowitz et al.; Lugo et al. [hereafter Pew 2013]; Tighe et al., *American Jewish Population Estimates: 2012*). The reasons for these differences are discussed in the academic literature in I. M. Sheskin and A. Dashefsky ("Jewish Population in the United States, 2006") and S. DellaPergola ("How Many Jews in the United States") and have been widely discussed in the Jewish press (see, for example, Zeveloff), but they hardly matter in the current context. Why? Because, even if the 5.4 million estimate on the low end is correct, in which case Jews represent 1.7% of Americans; or if the 6.8 million estimate is correct on the high end, in which case Jews represent 2.2%, it is difficult to imagine that the ability of the American Jewish community to influence public policy and elections is significantly impacted by the difference between these two percentages. For example, compare this approximately 2% with the population percentages for Hispanics (17%), for Blacks (13%), and for

Asians (5%) (United States Census Bureau). Even when viewed as a religious group, the 2% is dramatically smaller than evangelical Protestants at 26%, Catholics at 24%, mainline Protestants at 18%, and historically Black churches at 7% (Pew Forum on Religion and Public 2008). Jews are also a tiny minority compared to other assorted groups mentioned during elections, such as "soccer moms," suburbanites, the elderly, and baby boomers.

After discussing the relative merits of the various data sources employed in this paper, three main purposes are addressed. First, considering that Jews are such a minimal percentage of the American population, this study examines the reasons Jews play such a significant role in the American political system (Sheskin, "Why All the Emphasis on the Jewish vote?"). Second, issues related to political parties and American Jews' political ideology are discussed. Third, the reasons most Jews continue to vote Democratic, when other groups who have "made it" in American society have tended to become Republican, are addressed.

## DATA SOURCES

Much of this paper relies on data from: 1) the Pew Research Center Survey of Jewish Americans (Lugo et al.: hereafter Pew 2013); 2) the 2000–01 National Jewish Population Survey (NJPS 2000–01) (Kotler-Berkowitz et al.) sponsored by The Jewish Federations of North America (JFNA); and 3) local Jewish community studies sponsored by local Jewish federations (*Berman Jewish Databank*). All these studies have utilized the most advanced, and most expensive, methodology—state-of-the-art random digit dialing (RDD) telephone surveys.

The Pew Research Center 2013 survey (Pew 2013) completed 2,786 surveys with "Jews by Religion" and 689 surveys with "Jews of No Religion" for a total sample size of 3,475.

The sample size of NJPS 2000–01 is also larger than that for most other studies. For the "More Jewishly-Connected" sample in NJPS 2000–01, the sample size is 3,927; for persons who did not answer that their religion was Jewish, but were connected culturally or ethnically to the Jewish people ("Secular Jews"), the sample is 359, for a total sample size of 4,286. NJPS 2000–01 and the local Jewish community studies contain a much richer set of variables measuring religiosity than other studies. A drawback to the NJPS 2000–01 dataset is that these data are more than a decade old.

Many previous descriptions of America Jews' political behavior have relied upon the American Jewish Committee's (AJC) annual survey of American Jewish Public Opinion. While these surveys are a valuable source of information, particularly because of their time-series nature (that is, as data collected annually over decades), the AJC sample is not nearly as representative of American Jewry as the surveys employed in this paper (Perlman). One of the principal problems one encounters is that the AJC surveys generally only include interviews with Jews who state that their religion is Jewish, omitting many Jews (22% according to Pew 2013) who identify as being ethnically Jewish, but who would respond in a survey of religious identification that they are atheists, agnostics, of no religion, etc. (Kosmin and Keysar). The Workmen's Circle Survey and Jewish Values Survey (Cohen and Abrams) referenced below is based upon Internet surveys of randomly selected panels, but like the AJC surveys, cannot claim the randomness and sample size of Pew 2013 or NJPS 2000–01.

The problem with much of the data from such national polls as Gallup, Roper, and Quinnipiac is that, even when one thousand interviews with Americans are completed nationwide, given that Jews are only about 2% of the population, no more than about thirty Jews are usually interviewed.

While measuring the votes and opinions of persons who are known to have actually voted, exit polls often suffer from a small Jewish sample. Moreover, to obtain a satisfactory size for the Jewish sample, pollsters may oversample regions with heavy Jewish concentrations. For example, in Florida, pollsters often sample the largely Jewish Aventura area of north Miami-Dade County that is comprised mostly of retirees and immigrants from Israel, Russia, and Latin America. Jews living in such areas are often different demographically, religiously, and politically from Jews living in areas of lower Jewish density (Weisberg).

## PART I: THE REASONS JEWS PLAY A SIGNIFICANT ROLE IN AMERICAN POLITICS

### Geography and Demography

Two major reasons may be posited for the significant role Jews play in American politics. First, Jews are a much higher percentage of voters than they are of the American population. Second, the geographic concentration of Jews in a small number of states and the Electoral College system magnify the impact of the Jewish community at the national level, and the concentration of Jews in a few major cities and in a relatively small number of congressional districts is instrumental in providing the Jewish community with local impact.

While only about 2% of the American population, Jews form a higher percentage of the actual electorate for three reasons: First, about 81% of the members of Jewish households are of voting age, compared to 76% of all Americans. Second, Jews register to vote at a much higher percentage than do all Americans. About 90% of adults in Jewish households claim to be registered to vote (Sheskin, *Comparisons of Jewish Communities* Section 35; Lugo et al.) compared to about 64%–74% of all Americans. Third, registered Jews actually vote in a much higher percentage than do all Americans. According to the American National Election Study of 2008, 96% of Jews who were registered to vote actually did so, compared to 79% of Blacks and 76% of non-Jewish whites.

An analysis from the *New York Times* illustrates the impact. While Jews are only 2% of all Americans compared to 16% for Hispanics (in 2008), of about twenty million Hispanics who were eligible to vote in 2008, only about twelve million were registered to vote and only about nine million actually voted. Given the higher registration rate and voter turnout rate for Jews, the comparable figure for Jews may be about 4.5 million. Thus, although there are eight times as many Hispanics as Jews, there are likely only twice as many actual Hispanic voters, as compared to Jewish voters (Figure 1).

*Figure 1: Hispanic Voting over Time (see original chart at "The Hispanic Electorate").*

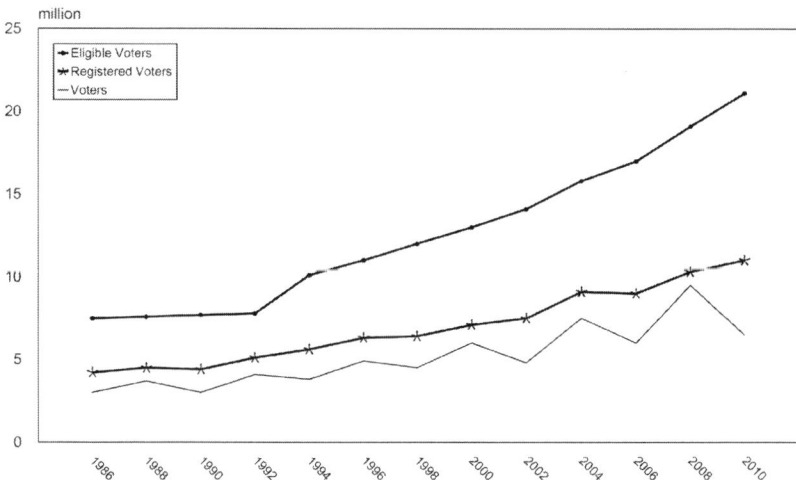

Jewish political influence in Presidential elections, however, derives not from being perhaps 3.5–4.0% of the national, voting electorate, but rather from the Electoral College, which effectively makes one's vote "worth more" in more populous states with more electoral votes. In 2013, 70% of Jews lived in just six states: New York, California, Florida, New Jersey, Illinois and Pennsylvania. Of the 270 electoral votes needed to be elected president, 149 are in these six states: New York with 9.0% Jewish, California with 3.2%, Florida with 3.3%, New Jersey with 5.7%, and Pennsylvania with 2.3% (Table 1). The top ten states for Jewish population have a total of 246 electoral votes. Thus, it is not the percentage of Jews nationwide, but their geographic concentration in several states that is important. For example, in the much disputed 2000 election between George W. Bush and Al Gore, had Florida not had a large Jewish population who voted overwhelmingly for Al Gore, the election would not have been in dispute.

The concentration of Jews in states with many electoral votes has increased over the past four decades, despite a small reduction in their overall geographic concentration. Table 2 shows the changes in the geographic distribution of Jews, by Census Region and Census Division, from 1971–2013, which, to some extent, reflects the changing geographic distribution of Americans in general. The percentage of Jews who live in the Northeast decreased from 63% in 1971 to 45% in 2013. The 12% who live in the Midwest remained virtually unchanged during this period, while the percentage living in the South increased from 12% to 21% and the percentage residing in the West increased from 13% to 24%. In sum, the Jewish population has shifted from the Northeast to the West and the South, with little change in the Midwest.

The final column of Table 2 shows that the number of Jews living in the Northeast decreased by 22% (822,000) from 1971–2013, the number in the Midwest decreased by 3% (22,000), but the number living in the South and the West each doubled from 1971–2013. The number of Jews residing in the South increased by 693,000 from 1971–2013 as the number in the West increased by 814,000.

From 1971–2013, significant increases were seen in the number of Jews in California (500,000), Florida (379,000), Georgia (102,000), Arizona (85,000), Nevada (73,000), Texas (71,000), Colorado (65,000), and Virginia (54,000). From 1972 to 2012, these eight states were allocated an additional fifty electoral votes, because of general population growth. The only significant decreases in Jewish population from 1971–2013 are seen in New York (minus 776,000) and Pennsylvania (minus 177,000). Their electoral votes were reduced by nineteen between 1972–2012, but both retain large Jewish populations. A statistically significant relationship is seen between the number of Jews and the number of electoral votes in a state (R = .711, alpha = .000).[1]

Examined in another way, of the five swing states in the 2012 presidential election with ten or more electoral votes, only Wisconsin (ten electoral votes, 28,000 Jews) does not have a significant Jewish population (Table 1).

For the 1972 presidential election, 73% of Jews lived in just five states: New York (13.8%), California (3.6%), Pennsylvania (4.0%), New Jersey (5.7%), and Illinois (2.5%). In 1972, these five states cast only 119 electoral votes, compared to the 149 votes that are cast by the top five states for Jewish population in 2013. Thus, the significant geographic shift of American Jews over the past four decades has actually concentrated Jews even more in states with many electoral votes.

Jewish political influence in Congressional elections is affected by geographic concentration within states. Examining the Jewish population in the top twenty Metropolitan Statistical Areas (MSAs) (Table 3), we see that 79% of Jews are concentrated in these twenty MSAs, compared to only 38% of the general population. Note as well that almost 65% of American Jews live in just seven MSAs (New York, Los Angeles, Miami, San Francisco, Chicago, Boston, and Washington, DC). Thus, Jews are concentrated within certain congressional districts (Paul). With many elections decided by less than five percentage points, Jews do have the ability to affect significantly election outcomes in these areas.

Jewish geographic concentration at the MSA level helps to explain the twelve Jewish Senators from ten different states and the twenty-six Jewish representatives from twenty-one different states elected to the 112th Congress (2011–13). Importantly, however, some Jewish Senators and Representatives were elected from states, such as Minnesota (0.8% Jewish), Oregon (1.0% Jewish), and Tennessee (0.3% Jewish), which actually have tiny Jewish populations. This is probably an indicator of a lessening of anti-Semitism in the US, as large numbers of non-Jews are clearly voting for Jewish candidates. Jewish politicians are not being elected "because they are Jewish" but for other reasons important to voters (see L. S. Maisel's discussion elsewhere in this volume).

Thus, the significant migration of American Jews over the past few decades has *not* dissipated American Jews' political influence, because as American Jews migrated, they mostly relocated to states with large numbers of electoral votes.

## Changes in the Size of the American Jewish Population

The 1990 National Jewish Population Survey (NJPS 1990) (Kosmin et al., *Highlights*) and NJPS 2000–01 suggest that the Jewish population *decreased* by about 5%, from 5.5 million in 1990 to 5.2 million in 2000, although a subsequent correction to the 2000–01 estimate by DellaPergola ("How Many Jews in the United States") suggests that the number did not decrease from 1990 to 2000. The estimates provided in the 1990 and 2000 *American Jewish Year Book* ("Jewish Population in the United States, 1989"; "Jewish Population in the United States, 1999") suggest that the Jewish population *increased* by about 3%, from 5.9 million in 1990 to 6.1 million in 2000. From 2000–13, Sheskin and Dashefsky ("Jewish Population in the United States, 2013") show a 10% increase in Jewish population, but attribute this not to an actual increase but to methodological improvements used to measure the US Jewish population. Using a meta-analysis of many US surveys, E. Tighe et al. (*Estimating the Jewish Population of the United States: 2000–2010*) found the same 10% increase as Sheskin and Dashefsky, but posited that the increase reflected a real change. This seems highly implausible, as the US white, non-Hispanic population increased by only 1.2% during the decade.[2]

In fact, if the Jewish population has remained about the same in recent years, or even if it has shown a small increase (as DellaPergola and Sheskin and Dashefsky posit), it is clear that the US Jewish population is likely to decrease in the future. First, in 2000, 16% of American Jews were elderly, compared to 12% for all Americans. Second, for a population to replace itself naturally, women need to average 2.15 children. According to NJPS 2000–01, Jewish women age forty to forty-four, that is, women at the end of their child-bearing years, average 1.86 children each, not all of whom are raised as Jews. According to Pew 2013, Jewish adults age forty to fifty-nine report an average of 1.9 children each (4.1 for Orthodox Jews, 1.8 for Conservative Jews, 1.7 for Reform Jews, and 1.4 for other Jews[3]). Thus, it is likely that the number of deaths in the Jewish community will continue to be higher than the number of Jewish births.

It is also likely that the number of Jews migrating into the US will continue to surpass the number leaving the country. To some extent, the large Jewish immigration from the former Soviet Union (FSU) has counteracted, until recently, the loss due to Jews "opting out" of being Jewish by simply rejecting their Jewish identity. In sum, while the Jewish population may have been relatively stable over the past decade, mostly due to the large number of FSU migrants, most observers believe that the Jewish population will decrease in the coming years, as it is unlikely that any significant immigration will occur to offset the losses resulting from more deaths than births and the number of persons who opt out in the future.

The likelihood of a future decrease in the US Jewish population certainly has political implications, although at least in the short run, the impact will probably not be significant. Given the Population Reference Bureau's estimate of 423 million Americans by 2050 (*Population Reference Bureau*), it is likely that only about 1.5% of Americans will be Jewish. On its face, such a decrease would imply a decrease in political influence, but for the same reasons that it currently may not matter whether Jews constitute 1.7% or 2.2% of the American population, so likewise, it may not matter if the percentage of Jews in the American population decreases to 1.5%.

## Other Reasons for Significant Jewish Political Influence

Two additional reasons may be posited for the significant influence of the Jewish community on the American political process: the political activism and significant financial contributions of the Jewish community and the inflated perception of the American public concerning the percentage of Americans who are Jewish.

The first reason for Jewish political influence is that Jews "are extremely active in American political life" (Wald and Calhoun-Brown 266). NJPS 2000–01 asked their Jewish respondents if they attended any political meetings or rallies, contributed money to a political party or candidate, or contacted or wrote a government official in the past year. About one-third of Jewish adults responded in the affirmative. In Washington, DC, for the same question, 45% responded affirmatively (Sheskin, *The Jewish Community Study of Greater Washington*) and in Bergen County (NJ), 34% did so (Sheskin, *The UJA Federation of Bergen County*). This political activism springs out of one of the guiding principles of Judaism—that humankind is God's partner in healing, repairing, improving and transforming the world; thus, by implication, Jews feel it is necessary to be involved in activities that do so. Helping Jews meet this obligation through political activism are numerous Jewish organizations which operate in the public square (Mittleman, Sarna, and Licht), such as the American Jewish Committee, the Anti-Defamation League, the Jewish Council for Public Affairs, the American-Israel Public Affairs Committee, the National Jewish Democratic Council, the Republican Jewish Coalition, and the World Jewish Congress.[4]

While reliable data are hard to find, it is significant that estimates of the percentage of total donations to the Democratic Party that derive from Jews range from "as much or more than about one-third" (Tobin) to "as much as 60%" (Edsall and Cooperman). Jewish money donated to the Republican Party is also significant, even without counting the millions donated by Sheldon Adelson, the Jewish Las Vegas casino mogul who was the largest single donor during the 2012 election cycle (Cline).

Second, non-Jews seem to have an inflated impression of the percentage of the US population who are Jewish. R. Nadeau, R. G. Niemi, and J. Levine (335) show that almost 40% of Americans think that 20% of the US population is Jewish and about 60% think that 10% or more is Jewish. Only 18% think that less than 5% of Americans are Jewish. More recent evidence (Herda) using the 2000 General Social Survey (GSS) shows that non-Hispanic whites estimate that 17% of Americans are Jewish; Blacks, 22%; and Hispanics, 20%.

## PART II: POLITICAL PARTIES AND POLITICAL IDEOLOGY OF AMERICAN JEWS

We now will examine the political party and political views of American Jews. Three important findings from this part should be emphasized. First, in 2013, the percentage of Jews who are Democrats (55%) or lean Democratic (15%) is 70%. The 55% Democratic in 2013 compares to 56% in 2000–01. The 13% Republican in 2013 compares to 15% in 2000–01. Thus, the recent claim of the Republican Jewish Coalition of an increase in Jewish Republicans is not borne out by the facts. It is also not true that younger Jews are more likely to be Republicans than older Jews, although the Orthodox are increasingly Republican, particularly during the Obama years. Also, 70% of Jews are Democratic/lean Democratic compared to 49% of all Americans (Table 4).

Second, from 2000–01 to 2013, the percentage liberal has decreased from 56% to 51% and the percentage Conservative has decreased from 23% to 19%. The percentage moderate has increased from 21% to 30%. Thus, there is also no evidence to support the belief that Jews are becoming more conservative. Also, in 2013, 51% of Jews are liberal compared to 22% of all Americans; 19% of Jews are Conservative compared to 40% of all Americans.

Third, the demographics of Democrats and Republicans and liberals and conservatives suggest that the current pattern, which indicates that the majority of Jews are Democrats and liberals, will not change in the foreseeable future.

**Political Party**

The generally held perception that American Jews are Democrats is shown to be mostly true (Table 4). Pew 2013 shows that 70% of Jews are either Democratic (or lean Democratic) while only 22% are Republican (or lean Republican) with 8% being independents or something else. The low percentage independent in the Pew survey may be due to the fact that the Pew data combine "Democrat" and "Lean Democrat" and "Republican" and "Lean Republican." In a first question, Pew respondents were asked: "In politics TODAY, do you consider yourself a Republican, Democrat, or independent?" In a second question, re-spondents selecting independent or volunteering no preference, other party, or don't know in the first question were asked: "As of today do you lean more to the Republican Party or more to the Democratic Party?" As measured by Pew, Jews are significantly less likely to be Republicans/lean Republican by 22% to 39% and much more likely to be Democrat/lean Democrat by 70% to 49%, than all Americans.

In Pew 2013, 78% of Jews of No Religion are Democrats or lean Democratic compared to 68% of Jews by Religion. About 24% of Jews by Religion are Republican or lean Republican, compared to 12% of Jews of No Religion.

NJPS 2000–01 asked: "Generally speaking, do you think of yourself as Republican, Democrat, independent, or something else?" Without the "encour-agement" that Pew used to move respondents out of the independent category, NJPS 2000–01 found that 56% of Jews are Democrats, 15% are Republicans, 22% are independents, and 7% are *something else* (Table 4). Jews are signifi-cantly less likely to be Republicans by 15% to 27%, much more likely to be Democrats by 56% to 31%, and much less likely to be independents by 22% to 40% than all Americans (Jones). These results are consistent with those of M. S. Mellman, A. Strauss, and K. D. Wald (15), who found that, for the 2000–08 Congressional elections, Jews were 28 percentage points more likely to vote for the Democratic candidate than were Americans in general. In addition, from 2004 to 2008, a noticeable increase was seen in Jewish support for Democratic Congressional candidates. A. Greenberg and K. D. Wald (174) discovered that between 1990 and 2000, only 39% of "white college-educated, urban middle-class non-Jews" identified as Democrats, compared to 60% of Jews with the same profile.

Note that the Republican percentage for the "Secular Jewish" sam-ple in NJPS 2000–01 is not significantly different from the "More Jewishly-Connected" sample, unlike in Pew 2013 where Jews by Religion were twice as likely to be Republican or lean Republican. The real difference is that the "Secular Jewish" group, reluctant to categorize their religion as Jewish, may also be reluctant to categorize their political preference, with 35% indicating they are independent and 15% providing a response categorized as "something else."

Table 4 presents these results as well as those of eight local Jewish community studies, which demonstrate that the Democratic percentage varies in the eight communities from 58% to 69% and the Republican percentage, from 8% to 15%. Thus, while it is true that a majority of Jews identify as Democrats, and only a small minority identify as Republicans, certainly not all Jews are Democrats. Moreover, significant numbers classify themselves as independents. Note that while differences do exist by community, Mellman, Strauss, and Wald (14) found that, at least since 1988, very little difference has existed in the percentage of Democratic voters across the four major geographic areas (Northeast, South, Midwest, and West).

In recent years, some Jewish Republicans have forwarded claims of significant increases among their number, particularly among younger Jews and Orthodox Jews. The Republican Jewish Coalition website states that "the last decade has seen tremendous growth in the number of Jews identifying with Republican ideas and the GOP"; however, no statistical evidence is offered to support this statement. In fact, the evidence is quite to the contrary. First, the 56% Democratic in NJPS 2000–01 compares to 55% Democratic in Pew 2013 (not including the "lean" percentages). The 15% Republican in NJPS 2000–01 compares to 13% Republican in Pew 2013 (not including the "lean" percentages). Second, Mellman, Strauss, and Wald (17) show that, based on exit polls, the percentage of Jews who self-identify as Republicans has been relatively stable. Figure 2 shows the self-identification of Jewish voters from 1972 to 2008. At least since 1980, with the exception of two years, self-identification as Republican has remained at 16% or lower. Thus, S. Windmueller's projection ("Are American Jews becoming Republican?") of an increase in Republican Jews is not borne out by these results, as Windmueller ("Revisiting the 2008 American Presidential Election") himself realizes in his analysis of the 2008 election.

*Figure 2: Self-Identified Partisanship among Jewish Voters, 1972-2008 (Mellman, Strauss, and Wald 17).*

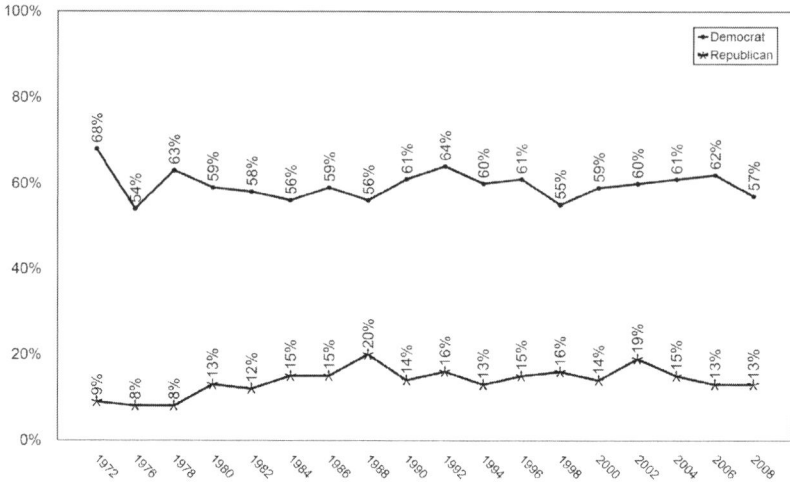

Likewise, the hypothesis that younger Jews are more likely to be Republicans than are older Jews is not supported by either Pew 2013 or the NJPS 2000–01findings, which suggest that nationally the percentage of Jews who are Republican is no different for younger Jews than for older Jews (Table 5). In fact, for Pew 2013, the lowest percentage Republican (17%) is for respondents age eighteen to twenty-nine. Among the eight local Jewish community studies, only those in Los Angeles (32%), Minneapolis (17%), and Bergen (22%) support the contention that younger Jews, those under age thirty-five, are more likely to be Republican and the Los Angeles data are quite dated (1997). In Bergen, this is because a large percentage of younger Jews are Orthodox. Hence, while younger Jews in some areas may be more likely to be Republican, such is not the case nationwide, either in 2000 or in 2013. Mellman, Strauss, and Wald (9) found that while for the period 2000–08, Jewish voters under thirty were less likely to vote Democratic than older Jews—75% for Jews under thirty, 77% for Jews thirty to sixty, and 84% for Jews sixty and over—Jewish voters under thirty have become *more* Democratic over time.

The claim of a greater percentage of Republicans among Orthodox Jews (Table 5) is verified by both Pew 2013 data (57%) and the NJPS 2000–01 data (25%) and is true as well in Washington (28%), Los Angeles (26%), the Twin Cities (Minneapolis/St. Paul) (45%), and San Francisco (19%). However, Orthodox Jews constitute only about 10% of all American Jews (Lugo et al.)

nationally, and while participation in Orthodox institutions appears to have increased in the past decade, the percentage of American Jews identifying as Orthodox has not changed significantly since 1971 (Massarik and Chenkin). Thus, even if Orthodox Jews were to become increasingly Republican, they are only a small minority of American Jews. The fact that more traditionally religious Jews, the Orthodox, are more likely to be Republican is consistent with the findings of R. D. Putnam and D. E. Campbell that religious voters tend to support the Republican Party. These results are also consistent with the findings of much earlier studies (Cohen; Cohen and Liebman). Interestingly, the Pew 2013 data show no statistically significant difference between percentage Republican for ultra-Orthodox (58%) and modern Orthodox (56%).

Why are Orthodox Jews identifying as Republican much more frequently than non-Orthodox Jews? First, Orthodox Jews are generally closer to the views of the Republican Party on the social issues. For example, while 82% of all Jews indicate in Pew 2013 that homosexuality should be accepted by society (as do 57% of all Americans), such is the case for only 32% of the Orthodox (20% of the ultra-Orthodox and 30% of the modern Orthodox). Second, Orthodox Jews are generally closer to the views of the Republican Party on economic matters. Pew 2013 shows that while 54% of all Jews indicate that they prefer a bigger government (as do 40% of all Americans), such is the case for only 34% of the Orthodox. Third, Orthodox Jews seem to be distrustful of Barack Obama, particularly with regard to his stance on Israel and Iran. While 60% of all Jews in Pew 2013 indicate approval of the way Obama is handling the nation's policy on Israel (as do 41% of all Americans), such is the case for only 36% of Orthodox Jews. While 52% of all Jews in Pew 2013 indicate approval of the way Obama is dealing with Iran (as do 45% of all Americans), such is the case for only 27% of Orthodox Jews.

NJPS 2000–01 results showed that 25% of Orthodox Jews identified as Republican compared to the 57% in Pew 2013. One possible explanation for this increase is that the distrust of Obama has caused the defection of Orthodox Jews from the Democratic Party. This suggests that when the Democratic Party is under different leadership, support by the Orthodox for the Republicans may wane.

The 2011 Jewish Community Study of New York (Cohen et al. 123) shows that the percentage of Jews who are Orthodox in the eight-county New York area (New York City, Long Island, and Westchester) increased significantly from 27% in 2002 to 32% in 2011. Because Orthodox fertility, and particularly ultra-Orthodox fertility, in New York is very high, 64% of Jewish children in New York are being raised in Orthodox households, many of them in ultra-Orthodox households. Since Orthodox Jews are more likely to be Conservative and Republican than are other Jews, this suggests that, at least in New York, one might expect to see an increase in Jews voting for Republicans in the future. This phenomenon will probably not be seen nationwide since, as noted, only about 10% of Jews nationwide are Orthodox and the percentage of ultra-Orthodox outside New York is very low.

      Figure 3 provides an alternative method for examining claims of a recent upsurge in Jewish Republicans. While it is true that the percentage of Jews voting for the Republican candidate in Presidential elections has increased recently from 16% for Bush in 1992 to 30% for Romney in 2012, the percentage of Jews voting for the Republican candidate from 1972–88 was, on average, 32%. So, one could argue that the recent increase from 16% to 30% merely returns that percentage to just below the average level from 1972–88. Moreover, voting for a Republican candidate does not necessarily mean that a particular voter identifies as a Republican.

*Figure 3: Percentage of Jews Voting for the Republican Candidate for President. In 1980, 19% of Jews voted for John Anderson; in 1992, 10% voted for Ross Perot (Weisberg for data through 2008. Due to methodological issues, two alternative histories are available: Maisel and Forman; and Mellman, Strauss, and Wald. While each presents slightly different results, the general pattern shown above prevails in both analyses).*

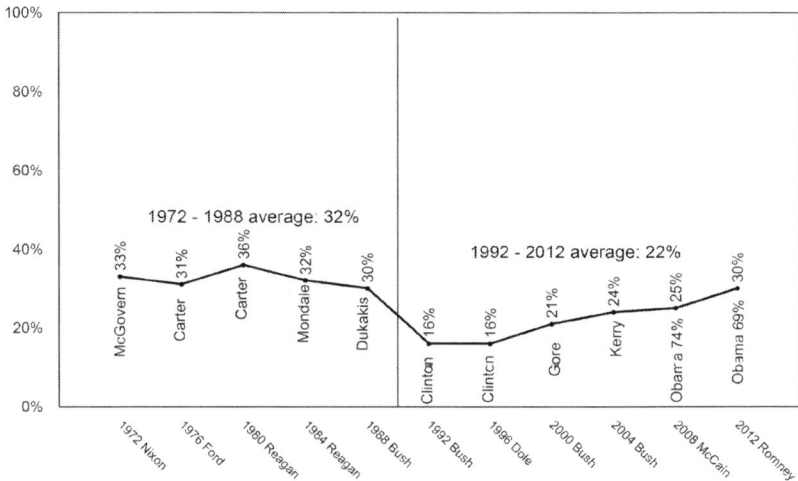

## Percentage Democratic by Demography and Religiosity

NJPS 2000–01 data allow further examination of the relationship between demographics and political party.[5] Overall, in 2000–01, 56% of Jews were Democrats. The Democratic percentage increased from 49% of persons under age thirty-five to 56% of persons aged thirty-five to sixty-four, 60% of persons aged sixty-five to seventy-four, and 68% of persons aged seventy-five and over. The decrease for the younger age cohorts does not, as shown above, imply an increase in younger Republicans. Rather, younger persons were more likely to indicate that they are "independent" or "something else."

This percentage was much higher for females (65%) than for males (46%). This result is consistent with Mellman, Strauss, and Wald (21), who discovered that in 2008 Jewish females were 18 percentage points more likely to self-identify as Democrats than were Jewish males. This "gender gap" is consistent with the gender gap for all Americans.

Fifty-one percent of respondents in Jewish households with children were Democrats, a percentage not much different from the overall percentage of Americans. To the extent that children follow their parents politically, this suggests that the Democratic percentage will be maintained in the future. N. Podhoretz (272) posits that all the evidence supports that political attitudes and affiliations have a strong correlation from parent to child.

The percentage of Jews identifying as Democrats increased from 46% of persons with no high school degree to about 53% of persons with a high school through a college degree and 63% of persons with a graduate degree. Mellman, Strauss, and Wald (11) also show that in 2008 Jews with a college degree were 14 percentage points more likely to vote for Obama than Jews without a college degree.

No variation was seen in the Democratic percentage by Jewish household income. This is consistent with the findings of Mellman, Strauss, and Wald (24), who found that no significant differences exist among income groups in the percentage of Jews who self-identify as Democratic between 1976 and 2008.

Orthodox Jews identified as Democrats (49%) at a much lower rate than Conservative (65%), Reconstructionist (66%), and Reform Jews (62%). Respondents from in-married households, that is households where both partners are Jewish, (64%) were more likely to be Democrats than respondents in intermarried households (45%). Since it is Jews in intermarried households who are least likely to be involved in Jewish causes and most likely not to raise their children as Jewish, this finding also suggests that the Democratic percentages of Jews will not change significantly in the foreseeable future.

Synagogue members (60%) and Jewish Community Center (JCC) members (61%) were no more likely to be Democratic than non-members (61% and 60%, respectively). Jewish organization members (66%), belonging, for example, to B'nai B'rith and Hadassah, were more likely to be Democratic than were non-members (58%). Donors to the local Jewish Federation in the past year (66%) were also more likely to be Democrats than non-donors (57%).

The findings concerning Jewish organization member households and Jewish Federation donors are, at first glance, not consistent with the findings by Mellman, Strauss, and Ward (12), which revealed that, in 2000, Jews who never attended synagogue services were 15 percentage points more likely to vote Democratic than Jews who attended services once per week or more.[6] This is no doubt because the vast majority of Jews who attend services weekly are Orthodox. Since, as noted above, the Orthodox are only about 10% of American Jews, when we examine the non-Orthodox, some evidence is seen that involved Jews were more likely to be Democrats than were less involved Jews.

### Percentage of Republicans by Demography and Religiosity

Overall, in 2000–01, 15% of Jews nationally were Republican. The percentage of Jewish Republican did not vary significantly by age, although the percentage was higher for males (18%) than for females (11%). In households with children, 18% of respondents were Republicans, a percentage not significantly different from the overall percentage. Again, to the extent that children adopt their parents' partisan identification, this suggests that the percentage Republican will maintain itself in the future. As noted above, this is likely to be different for the New York metropolitan area, where an increase in Orthodox Jews may well lead to an increase in Jews voting Republican, against the broader, national trend.

The percentage of Jews identifying as Republican was much higher for persons with no high school degree (27%) than for persons with a high school degree or higher (14%).

The Republican percentage was much higher for households earning $200,000 and over (25%) than for households earning under $200,000 (14%).

While 25% of Orthodox households were Republican, the 13% for Conservative households did not differ significantly from the 15% for Reform households. Only 5% of Reconstructionist households were Republican. Respondents in intermarried households (18%) were slightly more likely to be Republican than were respondents from in-married households (15%).

No significant differences were seen in the percentages identifying as Republican between synagogue, JCC, and Jewish organization members and non-members. The 12% of local Jewish Federation donors in the past year who identify as Republican was slightly less than the overall percentage (15%).

## Political Ideology

Pew 2013 shows that 51% of Jews identify as liberal, 30% as moderate and 19% as conservative. Jews by Religion (45%) are much less likely to be liberal than Jews of No Religion (68%) and are much more likely to be conservative (23%) than Jews of No Religion (11%).

The NJPS 2000–01data in Table 6 show that nationally 56% of Jews iden-tified themselves as liberal, 21% as moderate, and 23% as conservative. Unlike the case for political party and unlike the Pew 2013 data, the responses of "Secular Jews" differ little from the "More Jewishly-Connected" sample.

The percentage identifying as liberal increased from 47% in 1990 to 56% in 2000–01, but then decreased to 51% in 2013. The percentage identifying as conservative remained constant at about 22–23% from 1990–2000, but de-creased to 19% by 2013. The percentage identifying as moderate decreased, from 32% in 1990 to 21% in 2000–01, but then increased again to 30% in 2013.

For the six local communities in Table 6, the percentage self-identified as liberal varies from 47% to 63%, the percentage for conservative from 8% to 20%, and the percentage for moderate from 18% to 42%.

Mellman, Strauss, and Wald (19) found that, since 1976, at most 21% of Jews self-identified as conservative and that since 1996, with the exception of 2002, no more than 13% of American Jews identified themselves as conserva-tive.

As of Pew 2013, Jews are significantly more likely than are all Americans to be liberal by 51% to 22%, much less likely to be moderate by 30% to 38%, and much less likely to be conservative by 19% to 40%.

## Liberal Percentage by Demography and Religiosity

Using NJPS 2000–01 allows further examination of the relationship between demographics and political ideology. Overall, in 2000–01, 56% of Jews were liberal. This percentage did not vary significantly by age but was much higher for females (61%) than for males (51%).

Fifty-two percent of respondents in households with children were lib-eral, a percentage not much different from the overall percentage. To the extent that children follow their parents politically, this suggests that the percentage of liberals will be maintained in the future.

The percentage of liberals increased from 47% of persons with no high school degree and 43% with only a high school degree to 54% with some college or a two-year college degree, 58% with a four-year college degree, and 65% with a graduate degree.

The percentage of liberals was higher for households earning $25,000 and over (58%) than for households earning under $25,000 (50%).

Only 23% of Orthodox Jews identified themselves as liberal, compared to 64% of Reform, 50% of Conservative, and 83% of Reconstructionist Jews. Respondents in in-married household did not differ in percentage liberal from respondents in intermarried households.

Synagogue members (51%), JCC members (48%), and Jewish organization members (52%) were less likely to be liberal than were non-members (61%, 59%, and 58%, respectively). Local Jewish Federation donors in the past year were about as likely as non-donors to be liberal.

**Politically Conservative Percentage by Demography and Religiosity**

Overall, in NJPS 2000–01, 23% of Jews self-identified as politically conservative. The percentage increased from 19% of persons under age thirty-five to 26% aged thirty-five to sixty-four, but then decreased to 21% aged sixty-five to seventy-four and 17% aged seventy-five and over. The percentage is higher for males (26%) than for females (19%).

Twenty-five percent of respondents in households with children were conservative, a percentage not significantly different from the overall percentage. Again, to the extent that children follow their parents politically, this suggests that the percentage of Jewish conservatives will continue to be constant into the future.

The percentage of conservatives decreased from 30% of persons with no high school degree and 34% with only a high school or technical school degree to 24% with some college or a two-year degree, 20% with a four-year college degree, and 16% with a graduate degree.

The percentage of Jewish conservatives showed no correlation with household income.

Orthodox Jews (50%) were more likely to be politically conservative than were Conservative Jews (Conservative denomination) (26%), Reform Jews (17%), and Reconstructionist Jews (8%). Respondents from in-married households did not differ from respondents in intermarried households.

Synagogue members (26%) and JCC members (27%) were more likely to be conservative than were non-members (20% and 21%, respectively). Jewish organization members did not differ from non-members. The percentage of conservatives among local Jewish Federation donors in the past year was somewhat lower (20%) than among non-donors (24%).

Thus, none of the relationships between demographics and political party and political ideology suggest that any significant change in the political orientation of American Jews may be expected in the future. The data also suggest that most American Jews are as wedded to the Democratic Party and to liberalism, in general, as has been the case since 1928 (Podhoretz 258). Perhaps as important for American Jews as a whole is a recognition that, as of 2000–01, only 41% of Jews identified as liberal and Democratic, 10% as liberal and independent, and 9% as moderate and Democratic (Table 7). When representing their community, many Jewish leaders generally speak from a liberal Democratic viewpoint, which is the modal preference at 41%, but not the preference of a majority of American Jews.[8]

## PART III: THE REASONS MOST JEWS CONTINUE TO VOTE DEMOCRATIC

In the run-up to the 2012 election, the Republican Party and supporters such as the Republican Jewish Coalition expended an enormous amount of money and effort, attempting to overcome Jewish resistance to voting for conservatives and Republicans. This unprecedented targeted effort, partly funded by tens of millions of dollars donated by Las Vegas casino magnate Sheldon Adelson, led many to question whether Obama would lose a significant percentage of the Jewish voters who had supported him in 2008 (Sheskin, "Will US Jews Vote for Barack Obama in 2012?"). In fact, the Jewish vote for Obama decreased from 74% in 2008 to 69% in 2012. Given the small sample size for the 2012 data, the 69% in 2012 is within the statistical margin of error of the 2008 result of 74%.

To some extent, Jews defy the "natural progression" from the Democratic to Republican Party that at least some observers note for immigrant groups. The sociographer Milton Himmelfarb's aphorism that "Jews earn like Episcopalians, but vote like Puerto Ricans" (J. Berger, "Milton Himmelfarb, wry essayist, 87, dies") clearly applies. That is, one might expect that, as Jews have "made it" in American society, with a 2012 median income of $87,500 compared to $54,000 for all Americans, they would have become more conservative and vote for Republicans. Such has not happened. K. D. Wald and A. Calhoun-Brown (266) state that: "Collectively an affluent religious group, Jews nonetheless hold liberal political views that seem contrary to their economic self-interest."

At least five reasons may be posited for the persistent Democratic Jewish vote: the concepts of *tikkun olam* and *tzedaka*; the tendency of Jews to maintain their ideology over the ages; the Democratic/liberal urban environment in which most Jews reside; the movement of the Republican Party toward the religious right; and the ability of the Democratic Party to "control" its left wing, some of whom tend to be anti-Israel.

First, two concepts from Jewish *culture* contribute to the Jewish population's continuing Democratic and liberal viewpoints. The first concept, alluded to previously, is *tikkun olam*, a Hebrew phrase from the Talmud that means "repairing the world" and implies that it is humanity's shared responsibility with God to repair, heal, transform, and perfect the world. The second concept is *tzedakah*, sometimes translated as "charity," but really meaning "justice." Jews are commanded to "uphold the rights of the orphan; defend the cause of the widow" (Isa. 1:17) and in general to do justice by taking care of those less fortunate. The 2012 Jewish Values Survey suggests that 72% of American Jews see *tikkun olam* as a somewhat or very important value and more than 80% see *tzedakah* as a somewhat or very important value that informs their political beliefs and activities (Jones and Cox). Podhoretz (277), however, takes issue with the contention that Jewish liberalism springs from these concepts, noting that those who are most observant, the Orthodox, are also the most conservative (Lazerwitz, Winter, and Dashefsky). Jews have always felt that the ideals and positions of the Democratic Party better represent *tikkun olam* and *tzedakah* than those of the Republican Party.

Second, by virtue of the fact that they have clung to their identity for thousands of years, Jews have shown that they are a "stiff-necked" people (Exod. 32:9), that is, a stubborn people who, once committed to a particular path, will continue down that path. Perhaps "once a Jew, always a Jew" easily segues into "once a Democrat, always a Democrat." Jews were historically on the left of the political spectrum because more anti-Semitism sprang from the right than the left (Podhoretz 269). Podhoretz (282) goes on to posit that for many Jews, liberalism has replaced Judaism as their religion (Wald and Calhoun-Brown 266).

Third, as shown in Table 3, Jews overwhelmingly live in the nation's largest cities, areas that tend to be both Democratic and liberal. Living and working in an environment, in which Jews associate with others who share their Democratic and liberal standards, reinforces these values.

Fourth, changes in the Democratic and Republican parties themselves have provided an incentive for some Jews to remain within or even return to the former and turn away from the latter. As shown by Putnam and Campbell, decades ago one could find the highly "religious" in both political parties. More recently, Christian fundamentalists and evangelists have become the base of the Republican Party. While the organized Jewish community appreciates Republican support on issues related to Israel, the Democratic Party's core beliefs are much closer to those of the vast majority of American Jews on issues such as evolution, abortion, gay marriage, immigration, Medicare, the Affordable Care Act ("Obamacare"), Social Security, the government's role in the economy, and the use of diplomacy in international relations. Republicans of more recent vintage increasingly support matters like prayer in the public schools and, in a debate most thought was over, 2012 Republican Presidential candidate Rick Santorum even spoke out against birth control. Missouri Republican Senate candidate Todd Akin discussed "legitimate rape" and Richard Murdock indicated that pregnancies resulting from rape were events that God intended. Even though both comments were disavowed by Republican Presidential nominee Mitt Romney, many Jews had difficulty finding a "home" in a party that: 1) includes spokespersons espousing such points of view (Schrag); 2) includes those with "tea party" views; and 3) nominates someone like Sarah Palin, whom many considered anti-intellectual (Rubin). Jews are also concerned by evangelical denominations' efforts to convert Jews to Christianity (Wald and Calhoun-Brown 273).

While Windmueller ("Jews and the Tea Party Movement") points to some Jewish support for Tea Party *ideas* based on a 2010 Pew Research Center study, he relates a statement by Fred Zeidman, a Jewish Republican leader in Texas: "The idea of the Tea Parties scares the hell out of the Jewish community, and I can't tell you it's unjustified in some cases. There are some candidates out there that are clearly unqualified." In addition, Windmueller points to the neo-isolationism of some in the Tea Party as running counter to the pro-Israel agenda of the American Jewish community. Furthermore, B. Berkowitz points to the use of Holocaust imagery in an insensitive way by the Tea Party and the fact that some Tea Partiers have blamed Jews for the country's economic problems.

Differences between Jews and the base of the Republican Party are illustrated by the following examples. While 48% of Americans believe that evolution is the best explanation for the origin of life on earth, 77% of American Jews believe so (Pew Forum on Religion and Public Life 2008). While 52% of Americans favor allowing gay and lesbian couples to marry legally, 81% of American Jews support this (Public Religion Research Institute survey of March 2013). While 54% of all Americans think abortion should be legal in all or most cases (Pew Forum Survey of 2013), 90% of Jews support this.

A fifth reason Jews remain Democrats is that, even as some Democrats have moved further left, espousing support for racial and ethnic immigration quotas and harboring anti-Israel attitudes, the Democratic Party's leadership continues to reject these more extreme forms of radical-left ideology (Kotler-Berkowitz 135). Thus, for example, Jewish liberalism and Democratic Party membership have both pushed back against the rise of anti-Semitism that has occurred in some radical black circles (Wald and Calhoun-Brown 271).

Two counter trends to Democratic voting by the Jewish community may be noted. First, as mentioned above, the percentage of Jews who are Orthodox is liable to increase in the future and Orthodox Jews tend to vote Republican.

Second, Jewish immigrants from the former Soviet Union (FSU), who together with their children now number about 500,000–700,000 and may constitute as much as 10% of American Jews (P. Berger, "How Many Russian Jews Are in the U.S.?"), have tended to vote Republican as their FSU background has tended to set them against big government. They hold conservative views on taxes and Israel (to which many of them have very strong emotional attachments) which outweigh their more liberal views on the social issues (J. Berger, "Among New York's Soviet Immigrants, Affinity for G.O.P."). But, ameliorating this source of Republican votes is that the children of these Russian-speaking immigrants are tending to vote Democratic (Simpson).

## Voting Democratic in 2012

Most arguments made by Republicans during the 2012 Presidential election to sway Jews to vote for their ticket revolved around Obama's actions and views on Israel and, in particular, that he had not, as President, visited Israel during his first term. While one could certainly attribute some of the failure of the peace process during Obama's first term to the White House, other charges are more questionable. Though Obama visited Israel before becoming President, it is true that he did not travel there during his first term. But this was also the case for Republican Presidents Nixon, Ford, Reagan, and George H. W. Bush. Moreover, George W. Bush failed to visit the Holy Land until his eighth year in office. Also in play was the "cold" relationship between Obama and Israeli

Prime Minister Netanyahu; yet, Obama's policies benefitted Israel sufficiently to lead Israeli Defense Minister, and former Prime Minister, Ehud Barak to state, "I can hardly remember a better period of American support and backing" (Atterman).

But these arguments are, in fact, not all that relevant to American Jews' ultimate voting decision, as they do not vote solely, or even mainly, on the issue of Israel. In an American Jewish Committee survey of fifteen issues before the 2008 presidential election, Jews ranked Israel as the eighth most important issue behind, among others, health care, gas prices, energy, taxes, and education. When asked to name their top three issues, only 15%, mostly Orthodox Jews, chose Israel as one of the three. This does not mean that American Jews do not care about Israel or a candidate's Israel policy. They do. Pew 2013 shows that 69% of American Jews are very or somewhat attached to Israel (the same percentage as in NJPS 2000–01) and only 9% are not at all attached. According to Pew 2013, about 43% of American Jews have visited Israel. Thus, while American Jews are attached to Israel, they have not yet perceived enough of a difference in the candidates' positions on Israel so that the issue would surface and play a significant role in their choice.

In the Workmen's Circle/Arbeter Ring 2012 American Jews' Political Values Survey (Cohen and Abrams), three main groups of factors were found that influence Jewish voting:

a. A social justice commitment, including abortion, environment, same-sex marriage, and health insurance;
b. An economic justice commitment, including tax fairness, raising taxes on the affluent, the threat of banks, support for labor unions, and the need for government assistance to the poor;
c. Economic conservatism, including concern for high taxes, the business climate, and jobs.

A multiple regression analysis showed the following factors impacting the Jewish vote: party identification (.38), social issues (.27), economic justice (.21), economic conservatism (.12), and attachment to Israel (.07). The numbers in parentheses are standardized regression coefficients, and their relative values reflect the relative importance of each factor. Party identification is thus more than five times more important in determining votes than is the issue of Israel (Cohen and Abrams).

Note that almost all polls show that significant United States support for Israel derives, in part, from the backing of all Americans, not just American Jews. A poll released in March, 2013 revealed that American public support for Israel matched its all-time high (Saad, "Americans' Sympathies for Israel Match All-Time High"). In this poll, 64% of Americans sympathized more with the Israelis, while only 12% indicated support for the Palestinians, with the remainder (23%) indicating both, neither, or no opinion. Thus, of the 76% who have an opinion, 84% are pro-Israel. American support of Israel, then, is clearly not dependent on the approximately 2% of the population that is Jewish, but also upon Americans in general. Support for Israel tends, thus, to be bi-partisan.

## SUMMARY AND CONCLUSIONS

While there is no agreement on the number of Jews in the United States, nor whether that number is increasing or decreasing, it probably matters little in the ability of American Jews to influence the American political system, given their changed geographic distribution over the past four decades that has served to further enhance Jewish influence in the electoral process. Also contributing to their influence is the tendency for Jews to participate, both with time and money, in the democratic process.

The plurality of Jews is both liberal and Democratic, but Jews of all political stripes are evident. This finding is unlikely to change over the next generation. Nationwide, younger Jews are *not* more likely to be Republican, although such is the case in some local Jewish communities. Nationally and in some Jewish communities, Orthodox Jews are more likely to be Republican. Jews as a whole have not become more Republican.

For a variety of reasons related to history, Jewish cultural values, the differences between most Jews' positions on social issues and numerous core beliefs held by the contemporary base of the Republican Party, it is most probable that their overwhelming support of American Jews for the Democratic Party will continue. Even after the unprecedented spending of the Republican Party in 2012 to convince Jews to vote for Mitt Romney, the Jewish vote for Obama did not decrease appreciably. And perhaps most importantly, for the vast majority of the Jewish population, a candidate's stand on Israel is not the determining factor in their voting decision.

| Table 1 | | | | | |
|---------|---|---|---|---|---|
| **Jewish Population in the United States by State, 2013** | | | | | |
| State | Number of Jews | Total Population [a] | Percentage Jewish | % of Total US Jewish Population | Number of Electoral Votes |
| Alabama | 8,850 | 4,822,023 | 0.2% | 0.1% | 9 |
| Alaska | 6,175 | 731,449 | 0.8% | 0.1% | 3 |
| Arizona | 106,300 | 6,553,255 | 1.6% | 1.6% | 10 |
| Arkansas | 1,725 | 2,949,131 | 0.1% | 0.0% | 6 |
| California | 1,221,190 | 38,041,430 | 3.2% | 18.2% | 55 |
| Colorado | 91,920 | 5,187,582 | 1.8% | 1.4% | 9 |
| Connecticut | 116,050 | 3,590,347 | 3.2% | 1.7% | 7 |
| Delaware | 15,100 | 917,092 | 1.6% | 0.2% | 3 |
| DC | 28,000 | 632,323 | 4.4% | 0.4% | 3 |
| Florida | 638,985 [b] | 19,317,568 | 3.3% | 9.5% | 27 |
| Georgia | 127,470 | 9,919,945 | 1.3% | 1.9% | 15 |
| Hawaii | 7,280 | 1,392,313 | 0.5% | 0.1% | 4 |
| Idaho | 1,525 | 1,595,728 | 0.1% | 0.0% | 4 |
| Illinois | 297,985 | 12,875,255 | 2.3% | 4.4% | 21 |
| Indiana | 17,470 | 6,537,334 | 0.3% | 0.3% | 11 |
| Iowa | 6,240 | 3,074,186 | 0.2% | 0.1% | 7 |
| Kansas | 17,675 | 2,885,905 | 0.6% | 0.3% | 6 |
| Kentucky | 11,300 | 4,380,415 | 0.3% | 0.2% | 8 |
| Louisiana | 10,675 | 4,601,893 | 0.2% | 0.2% | 9 |
| Maine | 13,890 | 1,329,192 | 1.0% | 0.2% | 4 |
| Maryland | 238,200 | 5,884,563 | 4.0% | 3.5% | 10 |
| Massachusetts | 277,980 | 6,646,144 | 4.2% | 4.1% | 12 |
| Michigan | 82,270 | 9,883,360 | 0.8% | 1.2% | 17 |
| Minnesota | 45,635 | 5,379,139 | 0.8% | 0.7% | 10 |
| Mississippi | 1,525 | 2,984,926 | 0.1% | 0.0% | 6 |
| Missouri | 59,175 | 6,021,988 | 1.0% | 0.9% | 11 |
| Montana | 1,350 | 1,005,141 | 0.1% | 0.0% | 3 |
| Nebraska | 6,100 | 1,855,525 | 0.3% | 0.1% | 5 |
| Nevada | 76,300 | 2,758,931 | 2.8% | 1.1% | 5 |
| New Hampshire | 10,120 | 1,320,718 | 0.8% | 0.2% | 4 |
| New Jersey | 508,950 | 8,864,590 | 5.7% | 7.6% | 15 |
| New Mexico | 12,725 | 2,085,538 | 0.6% | 0.2% | 5 |
| New York | 1,760,220 | 19,570,261 | 9.0% | 26.2% | 31 |

| Table 1 |||||| |
| :--- | :--- | :--- | :--- | :--- | :--- |
| **Jewish Population in the United States by State, 2013** |||||| |
| State | Number of Jews | Total Population [a] | Percentage Jewish | % of Total US Jewish Population | Number of Electoral Votes |
| North Carolina | 31,675 | 9,752,073 | 0.3% | 0.5% | 15 |
| North Dakota | 400 | 699,628 | 0.1% | 0.0% | 3 |
| Ohio | 148,615 | 11,544,225 | 1.3% | 2.2% | 20 |
| Oklahoma | 4,625 | 3,814,820 | 0.1% | 0.1% | 7 |
| Oregon | 40,650 | 3,899,353 | 1.0% | 0.6% | 7 |
| Pennsylvania | 294,925 | 12,763,536 | 2.3% | 4.4% | 21 |
| Rhode Island | 18,750 | 1,050,292 | 1.8% | 0.3% | 4 |
| South Carolina | 13,570 | 4,723,723 | 0.3% | 0.2% | 8 |
| South Dakota | 345 | 833,354 | 0.0% | 0.0% | 3 |
| Tennessee | 19,575 | 6,456,243 | 0.3% | 0.3% | 11 |
| Texas | 138,705 | 26,059,203 | 0.5% | 2.1% | 34 |
| Utah | 5,650 | 2,855,287 | 0.2% | 0.1% | 5 |
| Vermont | 5,285 | 626,011 | 0.8% | 0.1% | 3 |
| Virginia | 95,240 | 8,185,867 | 1.2% | 1.4% | 13 |
| Washington | 45,885 | 6,897,012 | 0.7% | 0.7% | 11 |
| West Virginia | 2,310 | 1,855,413 | 0.1% | 0.0% | 5 |
| Wisconsin | 28,255 | 5,726,398 | 0.5% | 0.4% | 10 |
| Wyoming | 1,150 | 576,412 | 0.2% | 0.0% | 3 |
| Total | 6,721,965 | 313,914,040 | 2.1% | 100.0% | 538 |

Source: Sheskin and Dashefsky, "Jewish Population in the United States, 2013."
Note that the total number of American Jews is, conservatively, about 6.5 million
due to some double-counting between states (Sheskin and Dashefsky, "Jewish
Population in the United States, 2006").
[a] Source: <http://www.census.gov> (July 1, 2012 estimates).
[b] Excludes 77,675 Jews who live in Florida for three to seven months of the year
and are counted in their primary state of residence.

| **Table 2** **Changes in Jewish Population in the United States** **by Census Region and Census Division, 1971–2013** | | | | | |
|---|---|---|---|---|---|
| **Census Region/ Division** | **1971** | | **2013** | | **Percent- age Change** |
| | **Number of Jews** | **Percentage Distribution** | **Number of Jews** | **Percentage Distribution** | |
| **Northeast** | **3,828,135** | **63.2%** | **3,006,170** | **44.7%** | **(21.5)%** |
| Middle Atlantic | 3,420,265 | 56.4% | 2,564,095 | 38.1% | (25.0)% |
| New England | 407,870 | 6.7% | 442,075 | 6.6% | 8.4% |
| **Midwest** | **732,610** | **12.1%** | **710,165** | **10.6%** | **(3.1)%** |
| East North Central | 592,800 | 9.8% | 574,595 | 8.5% | (3.1)% |
| West North Central | 139,810 | 2.3% | 135,570 | 2.0% | (3.0)% |
| **South** | **694,850** | **11.5%** | **1,387,530** | **20.6%** | **99.7%** |
| East South Central | 41,425 | 0.7% | 41,250 | 0.6% | (0.4)% |
| South Atlantic | 560,835 | 9.3% | 1,190,550 | 17.7% | 112.3% |
| West South Central | 92,590 | 1.5% | 155,730 | 2.3% | 68.2% |
| **West** | **804,135** | **13.3%** | **1,618,100** | **24.1%** | **101.2%** |
| Mountain | 57,275 | 0.9% | 296,920 | 4.4% | 418.4% |
| Pacific | 746,860 | 12.3% | 1,321,180 | 19.7% | 76.9% |
| **Total** | **6,059,730** | **100.0%** | **6,721,965** | **100.0%** | **10.9%** |

Source: Sheskin and Dashefsky, "Jewish Population in the United States, 2013." Note that the total number of American Jews is, conservatively, about 6.5 million due to some double-counting between states (Sheskin and Dashefsky, "Jewish Population in the United States, 2006"). Also note that it is unlikely that the Jewish population of the United States has increased at the rate suggested by the table; rather, much of the increase shown may simply be due to improved data collection methods.

**Table 3**
**Jewish Population in**
**Top 20 Metropolitan Statistical Areas (MSAs)**
**in the United States, 2013**

| MSA Rank | MSA Name | Population Total [a] | Jewish | Percentage Jewish |
|---|---|---|---|---|
| 1 | New York-Northern New Jersey-Long Island, NY-NJ-PA | 19,831,858 | 2,067,500 | 10.4% |
| 2 | Los Angeles-Long Beach-Santa Ana, CA | 13,052,921 | 617,480 | 4.7% |
| 3 | Chicago-Joliet-Naperville, IL-IN-WI | 9,522,434 | 294,280 | 3.1% |
| 4 | Dallas-Fort Worth-Arlington, TX | 6,700,991 | 55,005 | 0.8% |
| 5 | Houston-Sugar Land-Baytown, TX | 6,177,035 | 45,640 | 0.7% |
| 6 | Philadelphia-Camden-Wilmington, PA-NJ-DE-MD | 6,018,800 | 275,850 | 4.6% |
| 7 | Washington-Arlington-Alexandria, DC-VA-MD-WV | 5,860,342 | 217,390 | 3.7% |
| 8 | Miami-Fort Lauderdale-Pompano Beach, FL | 5,762,717 | 555,125 | 9.6% |
| 9 | Atlanta-Sandy Springs-Marietta, GA | 5,457,831 | 119,800 | 2.2% |
| 0 | Boston-Cambridge-Quincy, MA-NH | 4,640,802 | 251,360 | 5.4% |
| 11 | San Francisco-Oakland-Fremont, CA | 4,455,560 | 295,850 | 6.6% |
| 12 | Riverside-San Bernardino-Ontario, CA | 4,350,096 | 22,625 | 0.5% |
| 13 | Phoenix-Mesa-Glendale, AZ | 4,329,534 | 82,900 | 1.9% |
| 14 | Detroit-Warren-Livonia, MI | 4,292,060 | 67,000 | 1.6% |
| 15 | Seattle-Tacoma-Bellevue, WA | 3,522,157 | 39,700 | 1.1% |
| 16 | Minneapolis-St. Paul-Bloomington, MN-WI | 3,422,264 | 44,500 | 1.3% |
| 17 | San Diego-Carlsbad-San Marcos, CA | 3,177,063 | 89,000 | 2.8% |
| 18 | Tampa-St. Petersburg-Clearwater, FL | 2,842,878 | 58,350 | 2.1% |
| 19 | St. Louis, MO-IL | 2,795,794 | 54,200 | 1.9% |
| 20 | Baltimore-Towson, MD | 2,753,149 | 115,400 | 4.2% |
| Total Population in Top 20 MSAs | | 118,966,286 | 5,293,080 | 4.4% |
| Total US Population | | 313,914,040 | 6,721,965 | 2.1% |
| Percentage of Population in Top 20 MSAs | | 37.9% | 78.7% | |

Source: Sheskin and Dashefsky, "Jewish Population in the United States, 2013."
[a] Source: <http://www.census.gov>.
Notes: 1) See <http://www.census.gov/population/metro/files/lists/2009/List1.
txt> for a list of the counties included in each MSA; 2) Total Jewish population
of 5,293,080 excludes 75,875 part-year residents who are included in MSAs 8, 12,
and 18; 3) The total number of American Jews is, conservatively, about 6.5 million
due to some double-counting between states (Sheskin and Dashefsky, "Jewish
Population in the United States, 2006").

**Table 4**
**Political Party**
**Community Comparisons**

Base: Jewish Respondents

| Community | Year | Republican | Democrat | Inde-pendent | Something Else |
|---|---|---|---|---|---|
| Washington | 2003 | 11% | 69 | 17 | 4 |
| Los Angeles | 1997 | 11% | 69 | 9 | 11 |
| Minneapolis | 2004 | 9% | 66 | 19 | 6 |
| St. Paul | 2004 | 13% | 63 | 18 | 6 |
| Bergen | 2001 | 11% | 63 | 19 | 6 |
| Seattle | 2000 | 8% | 63 | 25 | 4 |
| San Francisco | 2004 | 9% | 61 | 12 | 18 |
| Columbus | 2001 | 15% | 58 | 22 | 5 |
| NJPS (more Jewishly-connected) | 2000–01 | 14% | 61 | 20 | 6 |
| NJPS (secular Jews) | 2000–01 | 16% | 34 | 35 | 15 |
| NJPS (total sample) | 2000–01 | 15% | 56 | 22 | 7 |
| Pew (Jews by religion) | 2013 | 24% | 68 | 8 | |
| Pew (Jews of no religion) | 2013 | 12% | 78 | 9 | |
| Pew (total sample) | 2013 | 22% | 70 | 8 | |
| US | 2012 | 27% | 31 | 40 | 2 |
| US (Pew) | 2013 | 39% | 49 | 12 | |

Source: Sheskin, *Comparisons of Jewish Communities* Section 35 at <http://www.jewishdatabank.org>. US 2012 data from Jones. Pew data from Lugo et al.

Note: 1) The Pew data combine "Democrat" and "Lean Democrat" and "Republican" and "Lean Republican." In a first question, respondents were asked: "In politics TODAY, do you consider yourself a Republican, Democrat, or independent?" In a second question, respondents selecting independent or volunteering no preference, other party, or don't know in the first question were asked: "As of today do you lean more to the Republican Party or more to the Democratic Party?" This may be the reason fewer independents appear in the Pew survey.

2) The Pew survey "Jews by Religion" can be equivalenced to the NJPS more Jewishly-connected sample and the Pew "Jews of No Religion" can be equivalenced to the NJPS secular Jews.

3) The 2012 US data reflect the question asked in NJPS 2000 and the local Jewish community studies, while the 2013 US data reflect the question asked by Pew.

**Table 5**
**Percentage Republican fo American Jews**

**Base: Jewish Respondents**

| Community | Year | Under 35 | 35-49 | 50-64 | 65-74 | 75 + | Orthodox |
|---|---|---|---|---|---|---|---|
| Washington | 2003 | 9% | 13% | 10% | 13% | 6% | 28% |
| Los Angeles | 1997 | 32% | 8% | 19% | 5% | 5% | 26% |
| Minneapolis | 2004 | 17% | 13% | 6% | 5% | 3% | 45% |
| St. Paul | 2004 | 8% | 19% | 7% | 16% | 10% | |
| Bergen | 2001 | 22% | 14% | 10% | 6% | 4% | 12% |
| San Francisco | 2004 | 12% | 8% | 8% | 7% | 13% | 19% |
| Columbus | 2001 | 18% | 13% | 19% | 12% | 5% | 17% |
| Seattle | 2000 | 0% | 13% | 28% | 2% | 2% | 9% |
| NJPS (total sample) | 2000–01 | 15% | 16% | 15% | 13% | 11% | 25% |
| Pew (total sample) | 2013 | 18–29 17% | 30–49 24 | 50–64 24 | 65 + 20 | | 57% |

Source: Sheskin, *Comparisons of Jewish Communities* Section 35 at <http://www.jewishdatabank.org>. Pew data from Lugo et al.

**Table 6**
**Political Ideology of American Jews**

Base: Jewish Respondents

| Community | Year | Liberal | Moderate | Conservative |
|---|---|---|---|---|
| Seattle | 2000 | 63% | 29 | 8 |
| Columbus | 2001 | 63% | 18 | 20 |
| San Francisco | 2004 | 59% | 28 | 12 |
| Washington | 2003 | 52% | 37 | 11 |
| Los Angeles | 1997 | 50% | 33 | 17 |
| Bergen | 2001 | 47% | 42 | 11 |
| NJPS | 1990 | 47% | 32 | 22 |
| NJPS (more Jewishly-connected) | 2000–01 | 56% | 21 | 22 |
| NJPS (secular Jews) | 2000–01 | 54% | 23 | 23 |
| NJPS (total sample) | 2000–01 | 56% | 21 | 23 |
| Pew (Jews by religion) | 2013 | 45% | 32 | 23 |
| Pew (Jews of no religion) | 2013 | 68% | 21 | 11 |
| Pew (Total sample) | 2013 | 51% | 30 | 19 |
|  |  |  |  |  |
| US | 2011 | 21% | 35 | 40 |
| US (Pew) | 2013 | 22% | 38 | 40 |

Source: Sheskin, *Comparisons of Jewish Communities* Section 35 at <http://www.jewishdatabank.org>.

Data on US 2011 from Saad, "Conservatives." Pew data from Lugo et al.

1) NJPS 2000–01 respondents were asked: "Do you consider yourself extremely liberal, liberal, slightly liberal, moderate, slightly conservative, conservative, or extremely conservative?" Pew respondents were asked: "In general, would you describe your political views as very conservative, conservative, moderate, liberal, or very liberal?"

2) The Pew survey "Jews by Religion" can be equivalenced to the NJPS more Jewishly-connected sample and the Pew "Jews of No Religion" can be equivalenced to the NJPS secular Jews.

**Table 7**
**Political Party and Political Ideology of American Jews**

 Base: Jewish Respondents

| Category | Percentage |
|---|---|
| Liberal Republican | 2% |
| Moderate Republican | 3 |
| Conservative Republican | 9 |
| Liberal Democrat | 41 |
| Moderate Democrat | 9 |
| Conservative Democrat | 7 |
| Liberal Independent | 10 |
| Moderate Independent | 7 |
| Conservative Independent | 5 |
| Other | 7 |
| Total | 100% |

Source: Calculated by author from the 2000–01 National Jewish Population Survey.

## Notes

1.  The Pearson correlation coefficient (R) varies from -1 to +1. A value of R = 0 indicates that no relationship exists between two variables. A value of R = +1 indicates that a perfect positive relationship exists between two variables. A value of R = -1 indicates that a perfect negative relationship exists between two variables. In a positive relationship, as the values of one variable increase, the values of the other variable also increase. In a negative relationship, as the values of one variable increase, the values of the other variable decrease.

    The alpha value tests whether a particular value of R is statistically significantly different from 0, in which case we can conclude that a relationship exists between two variables. Alpha gives the exact probability of being wrong in concluding that a relationship exists.

    In this case, we conclude that a positive relationship exists between the number of Jews and the number of electoral votes in a state (R = .711). That is, states with larger Jewish populations also have more electoral votes. In reaching this conclusion, we are 95% certain that we are taking less than 1 chance in 1,000 of erring in our conclusion (alpha = .000).

2.  Calculated by author from data available at United States Census Bureau.

3.  Note that Orthodox Jews are only 10% of the Jewish population. Thus, their high level of fertility has a relatively small impact on the total fertility rate for all Jews.

4.  For a relatively complete listing of Jewish organizations that advocate both for Jewish and general causes, see Sheskin and Dashefsky ("Jewish Population in the United States, 2013," ch. 10). Jewish political activism is further documented in Goldberg; Maisel and Forman; Medoff; and Feingold.

5.  While the Pew 2013 *report* is available as of this writing, the *data set* has not yet been made available to researchers, so the Pew data cannot be used for this analysis.

6.  Note that service attendance was the only religiosity variable available to Mellman, Strauss, and Ward. While the level of involvement in one's faith for Christian groups can be measured satisfactorily by church attendance, many Jews, while not synagogue members and while not attending synagogue services regularly, are involved in home religious practices (lighting candles on Friday night, attending a Passover Seder, etc.), that have no equivalent in the Christian world. In addition, other Jews, while not at all religious, are involved in Jewish life in an ethnic sense in their participation in Jewish cultural activities and in support of Israel.

7.  See N 5.

8.  For further analysis of the relationship between various aspects of Jewish ethnicity and political party and political ideology, see Kotler-Berkowitz.

## Works Cited

"American National Election Study of 2008." *American National Election Studies.* 12 Oct. 2013 <http://www.electionstudies.org>.

Attermann, Jason. "Ehud Barak Corrects Fox News Host on Obama's Support for Israel." *NJDC.com.* National Jewish Democratic Council. 4 Aug. 2011. 12 Oct. 2013 < http://www.njdc.org/blog/post/BarakCorrectsGreta080411>.

Berger, Joseph. "Milton Himmelfarb, Wry Essayist, 87, Dies." *The New York Times* 15 Jan. 2006.

————. "Among New York's Soviet Immigrants, Affinity for G.O.P." *The New York Times* 8 May 2012.

Berger, Paul. "How Many Russian Jews Are in the U.S.?" *The Forward.* 25 Nov. 2011.

*Berman Jewish Databank.* A Project of the Jewish Federation of North America. 12 Oct. 2013 <http://www.jewishdatabank.org>.

Cline, Seth. "Sheldon Adelson Willing to Spend $100 Million to Beat Obama." *US News and World Report.* 14 June 2013. 14 Oct. 2013 <http://www.usnews.com/news/articles/2012/06/14/sheldon-adelson-willing-to-spend-100-million-to-beat-obama>.

Cohen, Steven M. *American Modernity and Jewish Identity.* New York: Tavistock, 1983.

Cohen, Steven M. and Charles S. Liebman. "American Jewish Liberalism: Unraveling the Strands." *Public Opinion Quarterly* 61 (1997): 405–30.

Cohen, Steven M. and Samuel Abrams. *Workmen's Circle/Arbiter Ring, 2012 American Jews' Political Values Survey.* 29 May 2013. Workmen's Circle. *BJPA.org.* Berman Jewish Policy Archive. 15 Oct. 2013 <http://www.bjpa.org/Publications/details.cfm?PublicationID=14166>.

Cohen, Steven M., Jacob B. Ukeles, Ron Miller, Pearl Beck, Svetlana Shmulyian, and David Dutwin. *Jewish Community Study of New York.* New York: UJA-Federation of New York, 2012.

DellaPergola, Sergio. "Was It the Demography: A Reassessment of US Jewish Population Estimates, 1945–2001." *Contemporary Jewry* 25.1 (2005): 85–131.

————. "World Jewish Population, 2013." *American Jewish Year Book 2013.* Vol. 113. Ed. Ira M. Sheskin and Arnold Dashefsky. Dordrecht: Springer Netherlands, 2013. 279–358.

————. "How Many Jews in the United States: The Demographic Perspective." *Contemporary Jewry* 33.1–2 (2013): 15–42.

Edsall, Thomas B. and Alan Cooperman. "GOP Uses Remarks to Court Jews." *Washington Post.* 13 March 2003, A01. 14 Oct. 2013 <http://www.stat.unc.edu/visitors/temp/NYT/Jcontrib.html>.

Feingold, Henry L. *Jewish Power in America: Myth and Reality.* Piscataway, NJ: Transaction, 2011.

Goldberg, Jonathan J. *Jewish Power: Inside the American Jewish Establishment.* Reading, MA: Perseus, 1997.

Greenberg, Anna and Wald, Kenneth D. "Still Liberal After All These Years?" *Jews in American Politics*. Ed. L. Sandy Maisel and Ira Forman. Lanham: Rowman & Littlefield, 2001.

Herda, Daniel. "Innocuous Ignorance? Perceptions of the American Jewish Population Size." *Contemporary Jewry* 33 (2013): 1–15.

"The Hispanic Electorate." *New York Times* 9 June 2013. 12 Oct. 2013 <http://www.nytimes.com/interactive/2012/06/09/us/politics/the-hispanic-electorate.html?ref=politics>.

"Jewish Population in the United States, 1989 (American Jewish Year Book 1990)." *Berman Jewish Databank*. 12 Oct. 2013 <http://www.jewishdatabank.org/Studies/details.cfm?StudyID=683 >.

"Jewish Population in the United States, 1999 (American Jewish Year Book 2000)." *Berman Jewish Databank*. 12 Oct. 2013 <http://www.jewishdatabank.org/Studies/details.cfm?StudyID=694>.

Jones, Jeffrey M. "Record-High 40% of Americans Identify as Independents in '11." *Gallup Politics*. 9 Jan. 2012. 14 Oct. 2013 < http://www.gallup.com/poll/151943/record-high-americans-identify-independents.aspx>.

Jones, Robert P. and Daniel Cox. *Chosen for What? Jewish Values in 2012, Findings from the 2012 Jewish Values Survey*. Washington, DC: Public Religion Research Institute, Inc., 2012.

Kosmin, Barry and Ariella Keysar. "American Jewish Secularism: Jewish Life Beyond the Synagogue." *American Jewish Year Book 2012*. Vols. 109–12. Ed. Arnold Dashefsky and Ira Sheskin. Dordrecht: Springer Netherlands, 2013. 3–54.

Kosmin, Barry A., Sidney Goldstein, Joseph Waksberg, Nava Lerer, Ariella Keysar, and Scheckner. *Highlights of the CJF 1990 National Jewish Population Survey*. New York: Council of Jewish Federations, 1991.

Kotler-Berkowitz, Laurence. "Ethnicity and Political Behavior among American Jews: Findings from the National Jewish Population Survey 2000–01." *Contemporary Jewry* 25 (2005): 132–57.

Kotler-Berkowitz, Laurence, Steven M. Cohen, Jonathan Ament, Vivian Klaff, Frank Mott, and Danielle Peckerman. *National Jewish Population Survey 2000-01: Strength, Challenge and Diversity in the American Jewish Population*. 2003. *The Jewish Federations of North America*. United Jewish Communities. 14 Oct. 2013 <http://www.jfna.org/NJPS>.

Lazerwitz, Bernard, J. Alan Winter, and Arnold Dashefsky. "Localism, Religiosity, Orthodoxy, and Liberalism: The Case of Jews in the United States." *Social Forces* 67 (1988): 229–42.

Lugo, L., A. Cooperman, and G. A. Smith. *A Portrait of Jewish Americans: Findings from a Pew Research Center Survey of U.S. Jews*. 2013. *Pew Research Religion & Public Life Project*. 14 Oct. 2013 <http://www.pewforum.org/files/2013/10/jewish-american-survey-full-report.pdf>.

Maisel, L. Sandy and Ira Forman, eds. *Jews in American Politics*. Lanham: Rowman & Littlefield, 2001.

Medoff, Rafael. *Jewish Americans and Political Participation: A Reference Handbook*. Santa Barbara: ABC CLIO, 2002.

Massarik, Fred and Alvin Chenkin. "United States National Jewish Population Study: A First Report." *American Jewish Year Book 1972*. Vol. 72. New York: American Jewish Committee and the Jewish Publication Society, 1973. 264–306.

Mellman, Mark S., Aaron Strauss, and Kenneth D. Wald. *Jewish American Voting Behavior 1972–2008: Just the Facts*. The Solomon Project. July 2012. *Berman Jewish Databank*. 14 Oct. 2013 <http://www.jewishdatabank.org/Studies/downloadFile.cfm?FileID=2857>.

Mittleman, Alan, Jonathan D. Sarna, and Robert Licht. *Jewish Polity and American Civil Society*. Lanham, MA: Rowman & Littlefield, 2002.

Nadeau, Richard, Richard G. Niemi, and Jeffrey Levine. "Innumeracy about Minority Populations." *Public Opinion Quarterly* 57.3 (1993): 332–47.

Paul, David M. *Jewish Population Survey of Congressional Districts: 2000 and 2006*. 2009. *Berman Jewish Databank*. 14 Oct. 2013 <http://www.jewishdatabank.org/Studies/details.cfm?StudyID=549>.

Perlman, Joel. *The American Jewish Committee's Annual Opinion Surveys: An Assessment of Sample Quality*. Annandale-on-Hudson, NY: The Levy Economics Institute of Bard College, 2007.

Pew Forum on Religion and Public Life 2008. "U.S. Religious Landscape Survey, Religious Affiliation: Diverse and Dynamic." Feb. 2008. *Pew Research Religion & Public Life Project*. 12 Oct. 2013 <http://religions.pewforum.org/pdf/report-religious-landscape-study-full.pdf>.

"A Portrait of Jewish Americans." 1 Oct. 2013. [Pew 2013] *Pew Research Religion & Public Life Project*. 12 Oct. 2013 <http://www.pewforum.org/2013/10/01/jewish-american-beliefs-attitudes-culture-survey/>.

Podhoretz, Norman. *Why Are Jews Liberals?* New York: Doubleday, 2009.

*Population Reference Bureau*. 12 Oct. 2013 <http://www.prb.org>.

Public Religion Research Institute. "Survey: Half of Americans Favor Federal Recognition of Same-sex Marriage." 22 March 2013. *Public Religion Research Institute*. 15 Oct. 2013 < http://publicreligion.org/research/2013/03/march-2013-religion-politics-tracking-survey/>.

Putnam, Robert D. and David E. Campbell. *American Grace: How Religion Divides and Unites Us*. New York: Simon & Schuster, 2012.

*Republican Jewish Coalition*. 12 Oct. 2013 <http://www.rjchq.org>.

Rubin, Jennifer. "Why Jews Hate Palin." *Commentary* Jan. 2010. 14 Oct. 2013 < http://www.commentarymagazine.com/article/why-jews-hate-palin/>.

Saad, Lydia. "Conservatives Remain the Largest Ideological Group in the U.S." *Gallup Politics*. 12 Jan. 2013. 14 Oct. 2013 <http://www.gallup.com/poll/152021/conservatives-remain-largest-ideological-group.aspx>.

———. "Americans' Sympathies for Israel Match All-Time High." *Gallup Politics*. 15 March 2013. 14 Oct. 2013 <http://www.gallup.com/poll/161387/americans-sympathies-israel-match-time-high.aspx>.

Schrag, Carl. "American Jews and Evangelical Christians: Anatomy of a Changing Relationship." *Jewish Political Studies Review* 17.1–2 (2005): 171–81.

Sheskin, Ira M. *The UJA Federation of Bergen County and North Hudson Community Study*. River Edge, NJ: The UJA Federation of Bergen County and North Hudson, 2002.

———. *The Jewish Community Study of Greater Washington*. Rockville, MD: The Kaplan Foundation, 2004.

———. "Four Questions about American Jewish Demography." *Jewish Political Studies Review* 20.1–2 (2008): 23–42.

———. "Why All the Emphasis on the Jewish Vote?" *St. Louis Jewish Light*. 24 Oct. 2012. 14 Oct. 2013 <http://www.stljewishlight.com/opinion/commentaries/article_3bf32bbc-1e00-11e2-a404-001a4bcf887a.html>.

———. "Will US Jews Vote for Barack Obama in 2012? *The Jerusalem Post* 21 March 2012.

———. *2013 Comparisons of Jewish Communities: A Compendium of Tables and Bar Charts*. 2013. Mandell Berman Institute, Berman Jewish Data Bank and The Jewish Federations of North America. *Berman Jewish Databank*. 15 Oct. 2013 <http://www.jewishdatabank.org/Studies/details.cfm?StudyID=595>.

Sheskin, Ira M. and Arnold Dashefsky. "Jewish Population in the United States, 2006." *American Jewish Year Book, 2006*. Vol. 106. Ed. David Singer and Lawrence Grossman. New York: American Jewish Committee, 2006. 133–93. 15 Oct. 2013 <http://www.bjpa.org/Publications/details.cfm?PublicationID=1347>.

"Jewish Population in the United States, 2013." *The American Jewish Year Book 2013*. Vol. 113. Ed. Arnold Dashefsky and Ira M. Sheskin. Dordrecht: Springer Netherlands, forthcoming 2013.

Tighe, Elizabeth, Leonard Saxe, Charles Kadushin, with Raquel Magidin de Kramer, Begli Nursahedov, Janet Aronson and Lynn Cherny. *Estimating the Jewish Population of the United States: 2000–2010*. Waltham, MA: Brandeis Univ., Steinhardt Social Research Institute, 2011. 15 Oct. 2013 <http://www.brandeis.edu/ssri/pdfs/EstimatingJewishPopUS042412.pdf>.

Tighe, Elizabeth, Leonard Saxe, Raquel Magidin de Kramer, and Daniel Parmer. *American Jewish Population Estimates: 2012*. Waltham, MA: Brandeis Univ., Steinhardt Social Research Institute, 2013. 15 Oct. 2013 <http://www.brandeis.edu/ssri/pdfs/AmJewishPopEst2012.pdf>.

Tobin, Jonathan. "Jews, Money, and 2012." *Commentary* March 2012. 15 Oct. 2013 <http://www.commentarymagazine.com/article/jews-money-and-2012/>.

United States Census Bureau. 28 Oct. 2013 <http://www.census.gov>.

Wald, Kenneth D. and Allison Calhoun-Brown. *Religion and Politics in the United States.* 6th ed. Lanham, MA: Roman & Littlefield, 2011.

Weisberg, Herbert F. "Reconsidering Jewish Presidential Voting Statistics." *Contemporary Jewry* 32.3 (2012): 215–36.

Windmueller, Steven. "Are American Jews Becoming Republican? Insights into Jewish Political Behavior." *Jerusalem Viewpoints* 509 (15 Dec. 2003). *Jerusalem Center for Public Affairs.* 15 Oct. 2013 <http://www.jcpa.org/jl/vp509.htm>.

Windmueller, Steven. "Revisiting the 2008 American Presidential Election: Reflections on the Jewish Vote." *Changing Jewish Communities* 44 (21 April 2009). *Jerusalem Center for Public Affairs.* 15 Oct. 2013 <http://jcpa.org/article/revisiting-the-2008-presidential-election-reflections-on-the-jewish-vote/>.

Windmueller, Steven. "Jews and the Tea Party Movement." *Sh'ma* 43 (1 Dec. 2012): 20–21.

Zeveloff, Naomi. "U.S. Jewish Population Pegged at 6 Million." *The Jewish Daily Forward.* 17 Jan. 2012. 9 July 2013 <http://forward.com/articles/149492>.

# American Jews and the Elephant Question*

## *Eric M. Uslaner*

My parents cried at their wedding.

Many people do, but these were tears of sorrow, not of joy. My parents were married on April 12, 1945. It was the saddest date in memory for American Jews. President Franklin D. Roosevelt died that day.

While Roosevelt's role in protecting Jews from the Holocaust is a matter of sharp debate, his strong opposition to Hitler played a key role in the conversion of Jews from Republicans to strong Democrats (Gamm 55 and ch. 2 more generally). For many Jews, Roosevelt was a hero. After a courtship in 1928 and 1932, American Jews became wedded to the Democratic Party (Weisberg 217, 221, 223).

At first glance, it may not seem so unusual that Jews became strong Democrats. So did most other immigrant groups—Irish, Italians, and Polish— as well as African-Americans. For most of these groups, the transforming figure was not Roosevelt, but New York Governor Al Smith, the first Catholic nominated for President—by the Democrats in 1928 (Key). Jews, like other minority groups, became part of the New Deal coalition.

So what makes Jewish voting behavior distinctive?

- Jewish support for Democratic candidates since 1936 has been overwhelming, ranging from 70% to 90% or more—in 1944 and 1964 (Weisberg 223).

- The New Deal coalition was formed among working class Catholics and poor blacks (Key). Jewish support for Democrats crossed class lines (Gamm 55).
- Conflicts over social and foreign policy divided the New Deal co-alition by the late 1960s and thereafter. So did economic issues as many urban workers entered the middle and upper-middle classes. The New Deal coalition had largely fallen apart by the Republican landslide of 1972—except for Jews, who remained loyal to the Democrats by more than two to one. Jews gave less support to Jimmy Carter in his reelection campaign against Ronald Reagan in 1980, but the President still got a plurality of the Jewish vote; and Jews returned to their "normal" two-to-one balance of support for Democrat Michael Dukakis in 1984 (Mellman, Strauss, and Wald 5).
- Even in 2010, when the Republicans swept the midterm elections, winning sixty-three new House seats, two-thirds of Jews backed the Democratic candidates (Gerstein 2).
- In 2012, Republicans believed that they had a strong chance to win a substantial share of the Jewish vote. They charged Democratic President Barack Obama with being insufficiently supportive of Israel. He had not visited the Jewish state. His relations with Israeli Prime Minister Binyamin Netanyahu were cool at best, while Republican nominee Mitt Romney had been a friend of Netanyahu since they were students at Harvard Business School. Republicans in Alabama and Mississippi believed that Obama was secretly a Muslim (Public Policy Polling). Jewish entrepreneur Sheldon Adelson spent up to $150 million of his own money in donations to Republican candidates—and at least $6 million to sway Jewish voters. Jews were a small share of the American electorate, mostly concentrated in states that Republicans couldn't dream of winning. But Florida has been very close in recent elections. No one knows for sure who car-ried it in 2000 and Obama barely took the state in 2008. Romney's staff also hoped to carry Pennsylvania—and Jews constituted 4% of each state's voters, enough to swing a close contest.
- In the end, neither Florida nor the national election was close. Obama won with only a small drop in his 2008 share of the Jewish vote.

These patterns suggest two questions:

1. Why is this voting bloc different from other voters? Why do Jews overwhelmingly support Democrats? And:
2. Why are Jews so persistently Democratic? Why, when some groups zig, do Jews zag?

The answers to these two queries are intertwined: Jews vote Democratic in part because they are liberal, but also because the Democratic Party has become the home of minorities who feel threatened by the Christian Right, which has become a central part of the Republican party base. The Christian Right touts its solidarity with Jews on the issue of Israel's security. Yet, historically Christian fundamentalists have held negative stereotypes about Jews, as I show below from surveys over the past fifty years. While anti-Semitism has declined among this group, it has not completely vanished. More critically, neither Jews nor fundamentalists feel at home with each other, either socially or in the same political coalition. These divisions have become more important in an era when partisan polarization is as much about tribal identity as it is about issue disagreement among partisans (Iyengar et al.). In an era when the historic divide between church and state appears threatened, the divisions between adherents of minority religions such as Jews (as well as Muslims) and evangelicals become politicized.

The strong support for Israel among many leading evangelicals/fundamentalists is not sufficient to win Jewish votes. American Jews are not as hawkish on issues of Middle East peace as are members of the Christian Right. And support for Israel has been bipartisan, so this issue has *not* become intertwined with issues of identity. Republicans sought to make Israel the critical issue for Jewish voters in 2012. They gained few (if any) votes on this issue and lost more on the cultural threat.

Politicians mistakenly believe that the key to the Jewish vote lies in where they stand on Israel. I shall show below that: (1) Jews do care about Israel; but (2) positions on the Middle East conflict are less important to Jews' vote-choice than are traditional party loyalties, domestic issues, and the concerns over identity (as argued by Iyengar et al.). Israel is not a central issue for Jewish voters because Middle East politics has not been marked by partisan divisions since the 1930s and because Jewish voters, in the main, make their decisions much as non-Jewish voters do—the state of the economy and domestic issues (Sigelman). I will now show support for each of these claims.

## WHY ARE JEWS DEMOCRATS?

The standard explanation for Jewish loyalty to the Democratic Party is that Jews are liberal, the Democratic party is liberal, so this is a straightforward match of policy preferences (Cohen, Abrams, and Veinstein). Yet Jews are not distinctively liberal across issues. They are more liberal on social issues (abortion, sexual morality, civil liberties, and church-state relations), but do not stand out on government spending, even on social programs (T. W. Smith, *Jewish Distinctiveness in America: A Statistical Portrait* 18–60). Lee Sigelman shows that Jewish voting patterns largely mirror those of other Americans. Kenneth Wald argues that there is nothing in Jewish experience that leads them to be liberal across contexts: In many countries, including Israel, Jews have either vacillated between the left and the right or backed mostly conservative parties (cf. Medding).

So why do Jews consistently back the Democratic Party? Wald and Peter Medding argue that Jews support the political party that makes them feel most secure. While economically secure and politically influential, Jews nevertheless feel insecure as a religious minority that has often faced persecution. The separation of church and state and the attachment to Israel both represent security against threats to Jewish identity.

T. W. Smith (*Jewish Distinctiveness in America: A Statistical Portrait* 58–59) argues that ". . . Israel helps keep American Jews distinctive . . . this attachment [is not] expected to wane . . . since one's current religion makes the Israel connection fresh and relevant, not merely ancestral and historical. . . . Jews differ more from Americans overall and from any other ethnic/racial or religious group . . . Jews are more unique than others." This "uniqueness" leads to a greater sense of vulnerability among Jews compared to most other minorities.

Identity and protection as a minority community is central to Jewish identity. In a country that is overwhelmingly Christian—and where a substantial number of Americans believe that *being a Christian* is central to being a good American (Thiess-Morse 86), the dividing line between church and state has become less clear. And this is when Jews feel least secure.

On the other hand, support for Israel in the Middle East conflict has been consistently strong. By margins ranging from five to one to ten to one, Americans support Israel over the Arab countries (Bard; Jewish Virtual Library, "American Public Opinion Polls"). While backing for Israel has dropped among liberal Democrats, a plurality still supports the Jewish State. Conservative Republicans and especially evangelicals back Israel by ratios of thirty-five to one or more (Pew Research Center for The People and The Press,

"Public Says U.S. Does Not Have Responsibility to Act in Syria"). Yet, there is at least plurality support for Israel among every demographic, religious, and age group. The Congress routinely enacts aid to Israel and passes pro-Israel resolutions almost unanimously.

With such bipartisan support for Israel, it is not surprising that there is mixed evidence on the importance of Israel as a voting cue for American Jews. In 2004, Jews who rated Israel as a most important voting issue, were 18% more likely to vote Republican than were Jewish voters who saw the issue as least important (Uslaner and Lichbach). This had a substantial impact. It "countered" the 18% gain Democrats won among Jewish voters who considered health care an important voting issue. How warm a Jewish voter felt toward Israel did *not* affect vote choice in 2004. Of nine issues in the National Jewish Democratic Survey Lichbach and I used, Israel ranked seventh in importance, with only abortion and separation of church and state with less concern.

The story was somewhat different in 2012. There was no evidence that Israel was an important voting issue in 2012—and any benefit received seemed to go to the Democrats. This is ironic for two reasons. First, Jewish support for the Democrats was greater in 2004 than in 2012. In 2004, the Democratic nominee, John Kerry, won almost 80% of the Jewish vote (Mellman, Strauss, and Wald 5). In national exit polls and the survey conducted by Gerstein, Bocian, and Agne for J Street in 2012, about 10% fewer Jews reported voting for the Democrat, Barack Obama (Uslaner).[1]

Second, there was a much greater effort by Republicans to win the Jewish vote in 2012 than in 2004. The Republican Jewish Coalition raised $6.5 million to support the party's nominees and other groups such as the Emergency Committee for Israel launched a series of television ads criticizing Obama (Lake). The group Secure America Now launched a series of television ads costing $1 million describing the Iranian nuclear threat and the tensions between Obama and Netanyahu (Siddiqui). The Republican Jewish Coalition sponsored an ad with a Jewish voter who had cast his ballot for Obama but would support Romney in 2012 because of conflicts with Netanyahu (Kessler), These ads were targeted at states and regions with large Jewish populations, especially where the election was likely to be close.

The Republicans gained little traction on Israel for three reasons: First, only a small share of Jewish voters (10%) saw Israel as one of the most important issues. Second, where Israel mattered for vote choice, the more dovish positions of American Jews bolstered Obama, not Romney. Third, the media blitz directed at Jewish voters had little effect on voters—and may have even backfired.

Voters who thought that Israel was the most important issue were no more likely to vote for Romney than the 90% of Jewish voters who did not put priority on Israel. Supporting an American role in peace talks did not matter either. However, two measures of Middle East policy did matter: Voters who opposed a Palestinian state and, who saw the United Nations as unfair to Israel, were more likely to vote Republican. But most Jewish voters (80.8%) favor a Palestinian state; even more (81.8%) want the United States to take an active role in peace talks, and over half said that the United Nations was fair to Israel (50.2%). So the President actually won Jewish votes on the Middle East issues. The television ads did not help Romney: People who saw the ads were almost equally divided on whether Netanyahu favored Romney (18%) or Obama (15%). Forty-four percent of Jewish voters saw the ads and were no more likely to vote for one candidate over the other.

The 2012 findings may be more telling than the 2004 results. The survey questions in 2012 focused on attitudes about Israel and the Palestinians, rather than the simple importance of Israel as an issue. In 2012, the importance of Israel played no role in the choice of Jewish voters. Nor did positions on the Middle East play a role in vote change from 2008 to 2012. The very small number of Jews who voted for Obama in 2008 and switched to Romney in 2012 seemed motivated almost exclusively by the weak state of the economy. Israel was not a factor.

T. W. Smith may well be correct when he argues that Jews have special ties to Israel that are different from those of other ethnic groups—or of the full electorate. However, these connections do not explain either why Jews have been Democrats or especially why they remain Democrats. It was a Democratic President—Harry S. Truman—who supported the creation of the State of Israel in 1948. Yet Republicans also backed the new state. Israel has not been an issue of partisan conflict in the United States. Romney and the Republicans tried to make it an issue dividing Republicans from Democrats. Yet, leading journalists (Heilmann), Israeli politicians such as Defense Minister Ehud Barak (Ovadia), and Democratic office-holders such as Rep. Debbie Wasserman-Shultz and former Rep. Robert Wexler, both Jews from Florida, argued that Obama was also a strong supporter of Israel. In the end, the charges that the President was weak on Israel did not pay off for the Republicans.

Attachment to Israel may make Jews distinctive. It does not make them Democrats. Jews had become strong Democrats well before Israel achieved independence (Weisberg 223). Nor has support for Israel kept American Jews in the Democratic fold—or driven them away from it for more than a single election. Jimmy Carter was seen as less supportive of Israel than was Ronald Reagan in 1980 and only 44% of Jews voted Democratic that year. However, by 1984 Jews returned to the Democratic fold and have stayed loyal ever since.

## CHURCH AND STATE: WHAT MAKES JEWS LOYAL TO THE DEMOCRATIC PARTY

Even before the New Deal, even before Franklin D. Roosevelt became President, the Republican Party has been associated with a fine line between church and state. In 1884 Rev. Samuel D. Burchard, a New York preacher, warned that the Democrats' close ties to Irish immigrant groups in his city, made them and their nominee, Grover Cleveland, the party of "Rum, Romanism, and Rebellion" (McNamara, 2012). Both parties, and especially the Democrats, were linked to the Ku Klux Klan in the first two decades of the twentieth century.

Once Roosevelt was elected, right-wing preachers took to the lecture circuit and to the radio to denounce the new President as the tool of Jews, and a likely Jew himself. The most prominent were the Catholic priest Charles Coughlin (History Matters) and Gerald L. K. Smith, a "nationalist, anti-Communist, anti-Jewish, pro-Christian" minister (Margolis). Both railed against Roosevelt and his ties to a presumed international Jewish conspiracy. Neither of them was connected to the Republican Party. But some Republican leaders—in and outside the Congress—favored a restrictive immigration policy and policies that favored "traditional Americanism." Republican Party chairman Henry P. Fletcher and Reps. Hamilton Fish (NY) and Frederick Britten (IL) made explicitly anti-Semitic speeches in the early 1930s, attacking both Roosevelt and the only Jewish member of the Supreme Court, Felix Frankfurter (Breitman and Lichtman 63, 77). These strident attacks and the close ties of some preachers to the Nazi movement, cemented the sympathies of Jews to the Democratic Party.

While Coughlin was a Catholic, much of the anti-Semitism stemmed from evangelical preachers. And their adherents held similar views. I turn now to an examination of Americans' attitudes toward Jews across a range of surveys. I compare the views of fundamentalists, evangelicals, and born-again Christians to other (non-Jewish) Americans. Different surveys have different categorization of Christians. Fundamentalists are usually defined as believing that the Bible is the literal word of God (Kellstedt 6). Evangelicals and born-again Christians are terms in which people describe their own beliefs. While fundamentalists, evangelicals, and born-again Christians are distinct concepts and some people may identify with one label but not another, overall there are small differences among these groups on theological, social, or political issues (C. Smith, *American Evangelicalism* ch. 2; *Christian America* 197–225). American Jews see little difference when evaluating fundamentalists and evangelicals; they see both as part of the Christian Right (Uslaner and Lichbach).

One common measure for assessing feelings toward different groups is the feeling thermometer. The thermometer ratings range from 0 (very cold) to 100 (very warm). In Table 1 I present the available thermometer scores for fundamentalists and other Americans (excluding Jews). Overall, Americans give relatively high ratings to Jews, with thermometer scores well above the neutral point of fifty. There were scores for Jews in 1964 and 1968 but not again until 1988. In the two earliest data sets—from the American National Election Studies—fundamentalists had significantly lower scores than did other Americans. In the two data sets from the 1960s fundamentalists rated Jews significantly lower than did other Americans. The differences may not appear large (three to five points), but they are consistent with other data from the 1960s. By the 1980s, fundamentalists were as warmly disposed toward Jews as other Americans. In 1992 and in 2006 (for evangelicals, though not for fundamentalists), they were marginally more favorable to Jews. Overall, their views of Jews were not more positive than other Americans. This stands in contrast to the pronouncements of many Christian fundamentalists about their love for Israel and the Jewish people.

**TABLE 1**
**Feeling Thermometers About Jews among**
**Fundamentalists and Others 1964–2008**

| Year | Fundamentalists | Others |
|------|-----------------|--------|
| 1964 | 60.4* | 63.7 |
| 1968 | 61.9* | 66.4 |
| 1988 | 61.7 | 63.6 |
| 1992 | 65.7* | 63.7 |
| 2000 | 66.0 | 66.8 |
| 2004 | 68.1 | 66.8 |
| 2006 (Faith Matters, born again) | 58.2 | 59.0 |
| 2006 (Faith Matters, evangelicals) | 60.6* | 57.7 |
| 2008 | 64.9 | 64.1 |

*Statistically significant difference

All surveys are from the *American National Election Studies (ANES)* cumulative file except for the "Faith Matters Survey, 2006." The ANES data are available (data and codebooks) at <http://www.electionstudies.org/>. The Faith Matters data were gathered by Robert D. Putnam and David Campbell and can be accessed at <http://www.thearda.com/Archive/Files/Descriptions/FTHMATT.asp>.

While fundamentalists were only slightly less favorable to Jews on the feeling thermometer, more specific questions show less favorable views of Jews among fundamentalists in a 1964 survey of anti-Semitism by B'nai Brith (Glock, Selznick, Stark, and Steinberg). I present data from the survey in Table 2 below.

## TABLE 2
### Attitudes toward Jews Among Fundamentalists and Others
### In 1964 B'nai Brith Antisemitism Survey

| Question | Fundamentalists | Others |
|---|---|---|
| Sympathize more with Israel than Arab countries | 38.5 | 42.4 |
| Jews push where they are not wanted | 20.9 | 19.7 |
| Jews have too much power | 11.5 | 12.6 |
| Jews are more willing to use shady practices | 60.1* | 41.2 |
| Jews more loyal to Israel than to U.S. | 57.0* | 31.2 |
| Jews as honest as other businessmen | 66.1* | 72.3 |
| Jews have a lot of irritating faults | 53.9* | 45.0 |
| International banking controlled by Jews | 67.9* | 48.7 |
| Jews are becoming more like other Americans | 81.2* | 86.0 |
| Jews don't care what happens to anyone but Jews | 37.4* | 25.6 |
| Jews like to be at the head of things | 68.6* | 59.9 |
| Jews always stirring up trouble with their ideas | 17.0* | 11.1 |
| Jews stirred up trouble between whites and blacks | 21.3* | 15.1 |
| Jewish businessmen are so shrewd and tricky that other people don't have a fair chance. | 48.2* | 35.3 |
| Jews go out of their way to hire other Jews | 72.7* | 54.2 |
| If a Jew is excluded from a social club, should he realize that Christians have a right to their own clubs? | 87.3* | 79.0 |

*Statistically significant difference

On a wide variety of measures, fundamentalists have less favorable views of Jews than do other Americans. They are more likely to say that Jews are more willing to use shady practices, are more loyal to Israel than to the United States, they have a lot of irritating faults, and that Jewish businessmen are so shrewd and tricky that other people don't have a chance. On these issues the gaps between fundamentalists and other Americans is often large—and they are statistically significant (the results couldn't have occurred by chance). Fundamentalists also hold other negative stereotypes of Jews—and even when such views are a minority, they are still more prevalent among fundamentalists than among other Americans. Large majorities of Americans said that it was acceptable for clubs to admit only Christians as members and that Jews should realize this—but this view was even more pronounced among fundamentalists. While only 21% of fundamentalists held that Jews stirred up trouble between blacks and whites, this was larger than the 15% for other Americans. On a few issues, there was no difference between fundamentalists and others: whether Jews push where they are not wanted and whether Jews have too much power. In the 1960s fundamentalists were evenly marginally less supportive of Israel.

Things changed by 1981, when the Anti-Defamation League conducted another survey based upon the 1964 items. This survey included a self-identification item on whether a respondent is born again. Two things stand out in Table 3, where I present some results from this study. First, the overall level of anti-Semitism seems to have dropped substantially. On only three of the fourteen questions in the table is there majority support for an anti-Semitic position: Jews are more loyal to Israel, Jews like to be at the head of things, and Jews go out of their way to hire other Jews. On just six of fourteen questions is there a statistically significant difference between born-again Christians and other respondents. Even as the overall level of anti-Semitism has dropped, on some issues anti-Semitic views still prevail and overall born-again Christians are more likely to hold such attitudes. They are less likely than others to hold that Jews have a strong faith in God, more likely to say that Jews are stirring up trouble, and more likely to be bothered if a Jew is nominated for President.

## TABLE 3
### Attitudes toward Jews Among Born-Again Christians and Others
### In 1981 Anti-Defamation League Anti-Semitism Survey

| Question | Born again | Others |
|---|---|---|
| Jews push where they are not wanted | 19.4 | 17.9 |
| Jews have too much power in business | 32.3 | 38.2 |
| Jews are more willing to use shady practices | 33.6 | 30.6 |
| Jews more loyal to Israel than to U.S. | 58.7* | 40.4 |
| Jews as honest as other businessmen | 83.3 | 78.6 |
| Jews have a lot of irritating faults | 33.6* | 27.3 |
| International banking controlled by Jews | 46.1* | 40.9 |
| Jews have strong faith in God | 85.9* | 91.4 |
| Jews don't care what happens to anyone but Jews | 21.6 | 21.7 |
| Jews like to be at the head of things | 51.5 | 53.0 |
| Jews always stirring up trouble with their ideas | 17.7* | 11.3 |
| Jewish businessmen are so shrewd and tricky that other people don't have a fair chance. | 26.9 | 25.5 |
| Jews go out of their way to hire other Jews | 56.9 | 55.1 |
| Bothered if Jew nominated for President | 25.6* | 19.0 |

*Statistically significant difference
The data and codebook are available from "Anti-Semitism" <http://www.thearda. com/Archive/Files/Descriptions/ANTSEM81.asp>.

The American Jewish Committee sponsored a "Religious Right" survey in 1996. It included both self-identification as a born-again Christian and a question about belief in the Bible as the literal word of God (fundamentalists). The level of anti-Semitism is substantially reduced from the 1981 levels among fundamentalists, born-again Christians, and other Americans. Yet on seven of the eight measures in Table 4, the Christian Right—whether born again or fundamentalists—express more anti-Semitic attitudes. While fewer than 20% of either group argues that Jews still must answer for the killing of Christ, just 5% of other Americans agree. Three quarters of other Americans agree that

Jews do not need to convert to Christianity, while only a third of born again or fundamentalist Christians hold this view. Only 20% of the Religious Right believe that you can still go to heaven if you don't believe in Jesus, while almost two-thirds of other Americans hold this view. The share of fundamentalists (as well as born agains and evangelicals) saying that Jews can get into heaven was substantially higher in the 2006 Faith Matters survey (about 40%), but it was still almost half of what other Americans hold.

---

**TABLE 4**
**Attitudes toward Jews Among Born-Again Christians,**
**Fundamentalists, and Others**
**In 1996 American Jewish Committee Religious Right Survey**

| Question | Born again | Funda-mentalists | Others |
|---|---|---|---|
| Jews have too much influence in society | 11.0 | 10.5 | 12.5 |
| Jews are more willing to use shady practices | 11.7* | 12.6* | 7.4 |
| Jews choose money over people | 23.4* | 24.2* | 12.9 |
| Still go to heaven even if don't accept Jesus | 21.8* | 18.8* | 64.2 |
| Jews don't need to convert to Christianity | 36.0* | 33.1* | 73.9 |
| Jews still must answer for killing Christ | 16.3* | 18.1* | 5.2 |
| Jews and Christians have similar values | 83.2* | 82.4* | 91.0 |
| Would vote for qualified Jew for President | 91.0* | 90.2* | 96.0 |

*Statistically significant differences.
Other percentage based upon comparison to born again respondents.

---

There is a sharp drop in the share of the Religious Right holding that Jews are more willing to use shady business practices, from 60.1% in 1964 to 33.6% in 1981 to about 12% in 1996. However, other Americans had even steeper declines, so that only 7% agree with this stereotype in 1996. Overall, then, T. W. Smith ("The Religious Right" 250, 253) argues that member of the Religous Right "tend to take antithetical positions toward Jews more often than other

Americans do . . . [and] have higher anti-Jewish scores" on a scale encompassing stereotypes of Jews.

These attitudes toward Jews among Christian conservatives are reciprocated by American Jews. Even though the Jewish samples in the American National Election Studies (ANES) are very small (between twenty and forty respondents) from 1980 to 2000, they consistently show that Jews give far lower thermometer scores to both evangelicals (from 1980 to 1988) and Christian evangelicals (1988 to 2000) than do non-Jews. Jews rate, on average, both evangelicals and fundamentalists twenty to twenty-five points lower than non-Jews. In the 2004 National Jewish Democratic Council (NJDC) survey of Jewish voters, only 2% scored above the neutral point of fifty on the evangelical feeling thermometer. The mean score for the evangelical thermometer was 23.8, while non-Jews (in the ANES 2004 survey) rated Christian fundamentalists at 59.4 (Uslaner and Lichbach).

There was no question about the Christian Right in the 2012 J Street survey. However, there was a thermometer about the Tea Party. Tea Party supporters are more likely to be evangelicals and very religious, even compared to other Republicans (Abramowitz). Thirty-six percent of Tea Party supporters are evangelicals compared to 21% of the American population and 55% of Tea Party backers see the United States as a Christian nation, even more than evangelicals do (Jones and Cox 8–9). Jews rate the Tea Party about the same as they did evangelicals in 2004: the mean rating was twenty-four and just fourteen among those who voted for Obama. American Jews see the Tea Party and the Christian Right in the same light: the correlation between their views of the two groups is a very high .718 (from the 2012 Jewish Values Survey of the Public Religion Research Institute, provided by Daniel Cox of Public Religion Research Institute [PRRI]).

These negative evaluations of evangelicals and the Tea Party played a large role in the vote choice of Jews. In both 2004 and 2012 attitudes toward evangelicals/the Tea Party were the second most important factor shaping vote choice among American Jews. In 2004, Jews with the most negative views of evangelicals were 25% more likely to vote for Kerry than were those who had favorable attitudes toward evangelicals.

In 2012, negative evaluations of the Tea Party led to a 32% greater likelihood of voting for Obama. In both years a third of all Jews rated the evangelicals or the Tea Party at zero on a one to one hundred scale and half of all Jewish voters rated each group at ten or less. The Christian Right repelled American Jews. And this was not just an issue of issue disagreement. The 2004 survey included policy positions on gay marriage, abortion, the National Rifle Association, and health care. The 2012 survey did not have such measures, but there was a measure on the importance of health care. It was not just the ideology of the Christian Right that repelled Jews. It was the commitment to a religious agenda and the threat to Jewish identity.

The salience of the Christian Right and the Tea Party to Jewish voters in 2004 and 2012 is ironic. Anti-Semitism has dropped sharply among Evangelicals. Republican Party leaders in the 1930s made explicit anti-Semitic statements. By 1944 the Republicans had shifted and endorsed Jewish migration to Israel (Breitman and Lichtman 258). By 1980 Ronald Reagan ran a strongly pro-Israel campaign against Democrat Jimmy Carter and in 2012 Romney portrayed himself as a better friend of Israel than Obama. Nevertheless, negative attitudes toward both evangelicals and Tea Party members are powerful determinants of the Jewish vote. Three factors seem to explain the strong negativity of Jews toward evangelicals and Tea Party members. First, in the 1960s Jews and evangelicals both voted for Democrats. In 2012, 78% of evangelicals cast their ballots for Romney.[2] Evangelicals comprised about half of the Republican Party's base in primary elections (Hirschkorn and De Pinto). Jews and evangelicals were now on opposite sides of the political fence. Second, over time cultural and social issues have become more important than economic concerns in shaping vote choice for President (Highton). So issues of identity have become more important. And, third, as Shanto Iyengar et al. have argued, American politics is now based to a large extent on tribal loyalties. Democrats don't want their children to marry Republicans—and vice versa, compared to the 1960s. Partisans are more likely to attribute negative stereotypes than they were fifty years ago: they see supporters of the other party as less intelligent and more selfish. The stronger attachment to one's own party, the more people are to see out-party supporters negatively. Jews are very loyal Democrats and evangelicals and Tea Party supporters are among the most steadfast Republicans. In this era of tribal politics, even reduced tensions over identity still matter a lot—especially when they may be based on historical conflicts between the groups.

## THE ELEPHANT AND THE JEWISH QUESTION

An old story goes (Levy):

> Four doctoral students—a German, a Frenchman, a Russian and a
> Jew—took a seminar requiring a paper about elephants. The German
> wrote about authority in elephant society. The Frenchman wrote
> about the love life of the elephant. The Russian wrote about shar-
> ing among elephants. And the Jew wrote about the elephant and the
> Jewish question.

The Republicans keep worrying about their elephant (the symbol of their
party) and the Jewish question: Why don't more Jews embrace the elephant?
We support Israel. We love them: 91% of Tea Party members say that they have
favorable views of Jews (from data provided by Daniel Cox of PRRI).

So why do these beliefs of Christian conservatives worry Jews—and lead
them into a renewed loyalty to the Democratic Party? They may love us, Jews
say, but for instrumental reasons. A strong Israel as a Jewish state is a prereq-
uisite for the Second Coming, as 59% of evangelicals believe that Israel represents the fulfillment of the biblical prophecy of the second coming of Jesus
Christ (Pew Research Center for the People and the Press, "Many Americans
Uneasy" 21). In the 2004 American evangelical survey by *Religion and Ethics
Newsweekly*, 86% of those who identified themselves as born-again Christians
held that it is important to convert non-Christians and over 90% of religious
conservatives (self-identified fundamentalists, evangelicals, charismatics, and
Pentacostals) said that it is important to spread their faith to others.[3]

It's not that Jews see the government as forcing them—or even pres-
suring them—to convert. Rather it's just that Jewish life has flourished where
there is a strong wall between church and state, where Jews can be Jews and
their children can be Jews. The transmission of Jewish values and identity from
generation to generation—*ldor va dor*—is essential to the continuation of the
faith. When the strong wall between the church and the state is weakened,
Jewish children will be exposed to Christian symbols in schools and other
public places. Before the Supreme Court outlawed prayer in public schools,
we started each day with the Lord's Prayer in the public elementary school I
attended, even though it was about 90% Jewish. I asked my Hebrew school
teacher why we didn't recite the prayer in our religious school. He looked at me
with a sarcastic grin: "It's a Christian prayer." I began to realize that this school
with an overwhelming Jewish student body had Christmas celebrations and a
special assembly for Easter—but nothing to mark any Jewish holidays.

The threat is not forced conversion, but rather the exposure of future generations to a theology Jews don't accept—because they are essentially strangers in their own country. Members of the Christian Right say that they love Israel and the data show that they rank Jews as highly as other Americans on the thermometers. Yet, they are still not comfortable with Jews keeping their faith. And for many Jews the evangelical "love" for Israel is just as a stepping-stone to the Second Coming, when Jews will be expected to convert to Christianity.

Evangelicals (and of course) the Tea Party are wedded to the Republican Party. But this hasn't always been the case. Evangelicals were heavily Democratic in 1964: 92% said that they voted for Lyndon B. Johnson, the Democratic nominee, and 85% identified with the Democratic Party. In 1964, evangelicals did not pose a political threat to American Jews. Both groups were on the same side, and there was thus no stimulus to provoke an identity-based vote. Evangelicals were not a well-organized political force in the 1960s (Uslaner and Lichbach). They became a political force in the 1980s—as they moved from a divided political bloc into a core element of the Republican coalition. As late as 1982, evangelicals split their votes evenly between the two parties. By later that decade, they split two-to-one for the Republicans, with their vote share rising to 70% or more by 2004 and to almost 80% in 2010 and 2012 ("Portrait of the Electorate"; "Exit Polls").

Jews stayed with the Democratic Party as other ethnic groups voted Republican because the issue that made Jews Democrats in the first place—a secure place in a country where they were a distinct minority—became more salient. As the Christian Right became an important force in the Republican Party, the ties of Jews to the Democrats were solidified. George H. W. Bush identified with the Christian Right—so Jews united behind Al Gore in 2000, whose Vice Presidential candidate was Jewish, and John Kerry in 2004, whose brother converted to Judaism and became a leading figure in the Boston Jewish community. Jews developed a particular affinity for Bill Clinton, who spoke two words of Hebrew (*shalom, haver,* "goodbye, friend") at Yitzhak Rabin's funeral and whose Cabinet was sometimes called "the *minyan,*" since it was so heavily Jewish. There are twenty-two Jewish members of the House of Representatives, 5% of the chamber; and eleven Jewish Senators ("American Public Opinion Polls"). Only one, House Majority Leader Eric Cantor, is a Republican.

In 2010 the Tea Party became a major force in the Republican Party; almost half of the Republican candidates for Congress were endorsed by at least one of the myriad Tea Party organizations (Bailey, Mumondo, and Noel 7). So as the bulk of the electorate zigged (toward the Republicans), the Jews zagged (remained loyal to the Democrats).

It is not just political conflict between Jews and evangelicals that keeps the former in the Democratic coalition. Jews feel comfortable among Democrats and Democrats feel comfortable among Jews. They feel personally uncomfortable among evangelicals, who don't know them very well. In the 2006 Faith Matters survey, just 19% of evangelicals had a close friend from any minority religion, compared to 35% of other Americans. It is not a one-way street. A third of Jews have close friends who are mainline Protestants and a similar share who are African-Americans. A quarter of Jews have good friends who are Asian or Hispanic and almost 60% are close to Catholics. But only 4% have strong ties to evangelicals.

Much of this aversion stems from Jewish perceptions that evangelicals don't understand them. In 1982, when I was a visiting professor at Hebrew University in Jerusalem, I traveled north and visited a beach at what Christians call the Sea of Galilee—and what Israelis call the *Kinneret* ("the Lake"). I met some American evangelical tourists who regaled me of their visit to the "Holy Land." They had spent two weeks in the country and had no contact with Israelis other than their tour guide. They seemed blissfully unconcerned that they were in a country that was a Jewish homeland—and had not visited any Jewish sites, not even the Western Wall. Perhaps they were atypical. Yet this story indicates the persistence of social distance between evangelicals and Jews.

Jews and evangelicals live in different worlds. And Jews worry that these worlds might collide. As the threat seems greater, you rally around the folks whom you believe will protect you. And you become very wary of the other side. You make love to a porcupine "very carefully," as the old expression goes. So the Jews make love to the elephant, very carefully and not very often.

## Notes

\*.   I am grateful to Jim Gerstein for sharing his 2012 data with me and to him and to Kerem Ozan Kalkan, Martin Kobren, Daniel Schnur, Kenneth Wald, Herb Weisberg, and Bruce Zuckerman for helpful comments and conversations. I am also grateful to Ira Forman of the National Jewish Democratic Council for providing their data on 2004 and to Patrick McCreesh of Greenberg Research for technical advice on the data set. I am also grateful for the very helpful comments of Beth Rosenson, Anna Greenberg, Karen Kaufmann, L. Sandy Maisel, John McTague, Alan S. Zuckerman (listed alphabetically), and especially Geoff Layman for comments on the 2009 paper. I am grateful to Jody Rose Platt and Anne Walter of the United States Department of State and Amnon Cavari of the Interdisciplinary Center (Herzilya, Israel) for arranging my attendance at the conference at the IDC where I first presented the 2012 results. I am especially grateful to Mark Gradstein and Dani Filc of Ben Gurion University of the Negev for sponsoring my visit to Israel, and to Mark Lichbach for discussions on our work on Jewish politics in the United States.

1.   See "2012 Fox News Exit Polls" for the national exit polls.
2.   See "2012 Fox News Exit Polls."
3.   See the data description at "America's Evangelicals."

## Works Cited

"2012 Fox News Exit Polls." *Fox News*. 2012. 21 Sept. 2013 <http://www.foxnews.com/politics/elections/2012-exit-poll/US/President> or <http://www.foxnews.com/politics/elections/2012-exit-poll>.

Abramowitz, Alan I. "Political Polarization and the Rise of the Tea Party Movement." Annual Meeting of the American Political Science Association, Seattle. 3 Sept. 2011.

*ANES: American National Election Studies*. 24 Sept. 2013 <http://www.electionstudies.org/>.

"America's Evangelicals." *The ARDA*. Association of Religion Data Archives. 24 Sept. 2013 <http://www.thearda.com/Archive/Files/Descriptions/EVANGEL.asp>.

"American Public Opinion Polls: Sympathy Toward Israel & the Arabs/Palestinians." *Jewish Virtual Library*. 2012. 24 Sept. 2013 <http://www.jewishvirtuallibrary.org/jsource/US-Israel/polls.html>.

"Anti-Semitism in the United States, 1981." *The ARDA*. Association of Religion Data Archives. 24 Sept. 2013 <http://www.thearda.com/Archive/Files/Descriptions/ANTSEM81.asp >.

Bailey, Michael A., Jonathan Mummolo, and Hans Noel. "Tea Party Influence: A Story of Activists and Elites." *American Politics Research* 25 June 2012. <http://www9.georgetown.edu/faculty/hcn4/Downloads/BMN_APR2012.PDF>.

Bard, Mitchell. "American Public Opinion Toward Israel." *Jewish Virtual Library*. 2012 (Updated May 2013). 19 Sept. 2013 <http://www.jewishvirtuallibrary.org/jsource/US-Israel/American_attitudes_toward_Israel.html>.

Breitman, Richard and Allan J. Lichtman. *FDR and the Jews*. Cambridge: Belknap of Harvard Univ., 2013.

Cohen, Steven M., Sam Abrams, and Judith Veinstein. "American Jews and the 2008 Presidential Election: As Democratic and Liberal as Ever?" *Berman Jewish Policy Archive: NYU Wagner*. 2008. <http://www.jewishdatabank.org/Reports/American_Jews_and_the_2008_Presidential_Election.pdf>.

"Exit Polls." *CNN Politics*. 10 Dec. 2012. 19 Sept. 2013 <http://www.cnn.com/election/2012/results/race/president>.

"Faith Matters Survey, 2006." *The ARDA*. Association of Religion Data Archives. 24 Sept. 2013 <http://www.thearda.com/Archive/Files/Descriptions/FTHMATT.asp>.

Gamm, Gerald H. *The Making of the New Deal Democrats: Voting Behavior and Realignment in Boston, 1920–1940*. Chicago: Univ. of Chicago, 1986.

Gerstein, Jim. "Making Sense of the Jewish Vote." Gerstein Bocain Agne. 28 Feb. 2012. 19 Sept. 2013 <http://jstreet-media-website.s3.amazonaws.com/JStreet_2012_Jewish_Vote_022812.pdf>.

Glock, Charles, Gertrude Selznick, Rodney Stark, and Stephen Steinberg. "Anti-Semitism in the United States." Computer file, 1964. Conducted by National Opinion Research Center, University of Chicago. ICPSR ed. Ann Arbor, MI: Inter-university

Consortium for Political and Social Research [producer and distributor], 1979.

Heilemann, John. "The Tsuris." *New York Magazine*. 29 Sept. 2011. 21 Sept. 2013 <http://nymag.com/news/politics/israel-2011-9/>.

Highton, Benjamin. "Sorting the American States into Red and Blue: Culture, Economics and the 2012 U.S. Presidential Election in Historical Context." Annual Meeting of the Midwest Political Science Association, Chicago. April 2013.

Hirshkorn, Phil and Jennifer DePinto. "White Evangelicals Are Half of GOP Primary Voters." *CBS News*. 23 March 2012. 21 Sept. 2013 <http://www.cbsnews.com/8301-503544_162-57398385-503544/white-evangelicals-are-half-of-gop-primary-voters/>.

Iyengar, Shanto, Gaurav Sood, and Yphtach Lelkes. "Affect Not Ideology: A Social Identity Perspective on Polarization." *Public Opinion Quarterly* 76 (2012): 405–31.

Jeansonne, Glen. "Gerald L.K. Smith Revisited: Liar, Racist, Demagogue—The Voice of a Generation." *David Margolis Journalism*. Sept. 2013. 21 Sept. 2013 <http://www.davidmargolis.com/article.php?id=31&cat_cc=6>.

"Jewish Members of Congress: 113th Congress." *Jewish Virtual Library*. 2013. <https://www.jewishvirtuallibrary.org/jsource/US-Israel/jewcong113.html>.

Jones, Robert P. and Daniel Cox. "Religion and The Tea Party in the 2010 Election." Washington, DC: Public Religion Research Institute. Oct. 2010. 21 Sept. 2013 <http://publicreligion.org/site/wp-content/uploads/2010/05/Religion-and-the-Tea-Party-in-the-2010-Election-American-Values-Survey.pdf>.

Key, V. O., Jr. "A Theory of Critical Elections." *Journal of Politics* 17 (1955): 3–18.

Lake, Eli. "Is Israel Mitt Romney's New Spring State?" *The Daily Beast*. 2 July 2012. 21 Sept. 2013 <http://www.thedailybeast.com/articles/2012/07/28/is-israel-mitt-romney-s-new-swing-state.html>.

Levy, Chava Willig. "The Kindle and the Jewish Question." *Orthodox Union*. N.d. 21 Sept. 2013 <http://www.ou.org/ou/print_this/55274>.

McNamara, Robert. "Newspaper Sunday: Rum, Romanism, and Rebellion." *About.com*, 19th Century History. 2012. 21 Sept. 2013 <http://history1800s.about.com/b/2012/09/30/newspaper-sunday-rum-romanism-and-rebellion.htm>.

Medding, Peter Y. "Towards a General Theory of Jewish Political Interests and Behaviour." *Jewish Journal of Sociology*, 19 (1977): 115–44.

Ovadia, Tomer. "Obama Praised by Ehud Barak on Israeli Security." *Politico*. 2012. 21 Sept. 2013 <http://www.politico.com/news/stories/0712/79162.html>.

Pew Forum on Religion and Public Life. "Faith on the Hill: The Religious Composition of the 113th Congress." 16 Nov. 2012. 21 Sept. 2013 <http://www.pewforum.org/government/faith-on-the-hill--the-religious-composition-of-the-113th-congress.aspx>.

Pew Research Center for The People and The Press. "Many Americans Uneasy with Mix of Religion and Politics." 24 Aug. 2006. 21 Sept. 2013 <http://people-press.org/reports/pdf/287.pdf>.

———. "Public Says U.S. Does Not Have Responsibility to Act in Syria: Israel Support

Unchanged in Wake of Gaza Conflict." 12 Dec. 2012. 21 Sept. 2013 <http://www.
people-press.org/2012/12/14/public-says-u-s-does-not-have-responsibility-to-act-
in-syria/1/>.

"Portrait of the Electorate: Table of Detailed Results." *New York Times*. 7 Nov. 2010. 21 Sept.
2013 <http://www.nytimes.com/interactive/2010/11/07/weekinreview/20101107-
detailed-exitpolls.html>.

Public Policy Polling. "Other Notes from Alabama and Mississippi." 12 March 2012. 21
Sept. 2013 <http://www.publicpolicypolling.com/main/2012/03/other-notes-from-
alabama-and-mississippi.html>.

Siddiqui, Sabrina. "Israel Prime Minister Bibi Netanyahu Used In Conservative Attack
Ad Against Obama." *The Huffington Post*. 20 Sept. 2012. 21 Sept. 2013 <http://www.
huffingtonpost.com/2012/09/20/netanyahu-obama-attack-ad_n_1901109.html>.

Sigelman, Lee. "If You Prick Us, Do We Not Bleed? If You Tickle Us, Do We Not Laugh?"
Jews and Pocketbook Voting." *Journal of Politics* 53 (1991): 977–92.

Smith, Christian. *American Evangelicalism: Embattled and Thriving*. Chicago: Univ. of
Chicago, 1998.

———. Christian America? What Evangelicals Really Want. Berkeley: Univ. of
California, 2000.

Smith, Tom W. *Jewish Distinctiveness in America: A Statistical Portrait*. New York:
American Jewish Committee, 1995. <http://www.jewishdatabank.org/Reports/
AJC_JewishDistinctivenessAmerica_TS_April2005.pdf>.

———. "The Religious Right and Anti-Semitism." *Review of Religious Research* 40
(1999): 244–58.

———. *Jewish Distinctiveness in America*. New York: American Jewish Committee,
2005.

"Somebody Must Be Blamed": Father Coughlin Speaks to the Nation." *History Matters*.
21 Sept. 2013 <http://historymatters.gmu.edu/d/5111/>.

Theiss-Morse, Elizabeth. *Who Counts as an American? The Boundaries of National
Identity*. New York: Cambridge Univ., 2009.

Uslaner, Eric M. "What's the Matter with Palm Beach County?" Conference on "The U.S.
Presidential Election: Campaign and Results," Interdisciplinary Center Herzilya,
Israel 6–7 Jan. 2013. 21 Sept. 2013 <http://portal.idc.ac.il/en/schools/Government/
US2012atIDC/Documents/Uslaner.pdf>.

Uslaner, Eric M. and Mark Lichbach. "Identity versus Identity: Israel and Evangelicals
and the Two Front War for Jewish Votes." *Politics and Religion*, 2 (2009): 395–419.

Wald, Kenneth D. "The Puzzling Politics of American Jewry." ARDA Guiding Paper
Series. 2010. State College, PA: The Association of Religion Data Archives at The
Pennsylvania State University. 21 Sept. 2013 <http://www.thearda.com/rrh/papers/
guidingpapers.asp>.

Weisberg, Herbert F. "Reconsidering Jewish Presidential Voting Statistics." *Contemporary
Jewry* 32 (2012): 215–36.

# Jewish Elected Officials for National Office, 1945–2013: From Representing Fellow Jews to Assimlated American Politicians

## *L. Sandy Maisel*

With the retirements of Herbert H. ("Herb") Kohl (D-WI) and Joseph I. ("Joe") Lieberman (I-CT) from the United States Senate and the retirements of Barney Frank (D-MA) and Gary Ackerman (D-NY) along with the defeat of Howard Berman (D-CA) from the US House of Representatives, Jewish legislators, who possessed 140 years of cumulative experience at the end of the 112th Congress, did not take their seats when the 113th Congress, convened in January, 2013. Many, who might have reason to worry about representation by Jews at the highest levels of government, expressed concern. Not only did these senior members of the United States Congress leave office, but the total number of Jews serving in the national legislative bodies also declined. When Barack Obama gave his first State of the Union address in 2009, twelve Jewish United States Senators and thirty-one Jewish Congressmen sat in the House Chamber to hear his speech. Four years later, nine Jewish Senators and only twenty-two House Members heard his fifth State of the Union, at the beginning of his second term.

The aim of this study is to examine the recent history of Jewish elected officials at the highest levels of the Federal Government. Its goal is to demarcate patterns that will show when and from where Jews have been elected to high public office, and, in light of these patterns, to put these recent elections into an appropriate context. Two important themes recur throughout this study.

The first is the importance of identity-politics, not just for Jewish politicians but for members of various ethnic groups who seek elective office.[1]
Identity politics refers to individuals engaging in political activity that is centered around their race, gender, religion, ethnicity, sexual orientation or similar categories as opposed to activity centered around social class or economic
distinctions. Jews have always taken pride in the accomplishments of other
Jews (and bemoaned activities by prominent Jews that call for derision). As will
be seen below, the extent to which Jewish identity is a critical factor in the electoral success and subsequent activities of Jewish politicians has evolved over
the period of this study; similarly how voters—Jews and non-Jews—respond to
Jewish candidates also changed during the time of this study.

The second theme relates to demographic representation. The American
political system is based on geographic representation; governors and legislators are elected from specific, geographically defined areas. But those elected
to office are also members of various demographic groups—men and women;
Catholics, Protestants, Jews, and Muslims, etc.; Blacks, Latinos, and Whites;
gays and straights; and others. While officials are not elected by these groups,
public officials who are members of these groups often feel that they represent those who share their demographic characteristics. Leaders who speak
for these groups think it important that they are represented in state capitals,
in the halls of Congress, and in other positions of power. They keep track of
how many members of their group hold these positions, and they turn to these
elected officials when issues involving the groups' identities are on the governing agenda.

Concern for this kind of representation, demographic representation,
is the cause for the alarm raised when so many Jewish Congressmen and
Senators left after the 112th Congress. However, despite that concern, a key
fact remains. Jews are over-represented, compared to their percentage in the
population, in the highest offices in this land—and they have been so for many
decades. That one statistic says nothing about who these Jews are, what areas
they represent, with what party they affiliate, or how they act once in office.
However, it stands in stark contrast to the demographic representation of most
other identifiable groups.

To develop these themes, we will be examining electoral patterns that
reveal how Jews have been elected as Governors, United States Senators, and
Representatives to the United States House of Representatives from the end
of World War II through the 2012 election. I have chosen to focus on these
offices, in particular, because of their significance and the availability of data.

Governors and United States Senators are the most prominent figures elected on a statewide basis; Congressmen represent smaller constituencies (except in those states with a single Member of Congress),[2] and thus one can say more about the effect of concentrated Jewish populations on electoral prospects.

The choice of timeframe for a study such as this one is always, to some extent, arbitrary, and this case is no different. Nonetheless, it has a reasonable rationale. Only five of the Jews elected governor or to the House or the Senate from 1932—the election often taken as the beginning of a new electoral period in our nation's history[3]—until World War Two continued to serve after the War; thus, to a large extent, this study begins with a fresh set of actors. The New Deal Coalition persisted for many years, thus providing a more or less constant political context. However, modern campaign techniques began to replace old-style machine politics, gradually and on an area-by-area basis, in the post-War period. And, as I will argue, the nature of electoral competition for Jews has also changed in significant ways in the last six decades—ways that could not be as well understood before now.

## DESCRIPTIVE REPRESENTATION

There are two separate but related lines of reasoning that lead one to conclude that a consideration of the careers of Jewish elected officials is worthy of close study. The first concerns issues of representation. We may pose the question regarding whether Jews have certain views on policy matters that are best represented by Jews. Descriptive representation calls for election of those who are "in their own persons and lives in some sense typical of the larger class of persons whom they represent" (Mansbridge 629). Descriptive representation is most often used to argue for the election of more minority candidates and/ or women, with the argument being that African-Americans or Hispanics or Asian-Americans are better able to represent the views of those who share their racial, ethnic, or gender characteristics than are those who do not.

So is the same premise applicable for Jews? Some would argue that it is, especially on issues relating to Israel. One could make similar arguments on church-state relations, on hate-speech, and perhaps on a number of other issues. One could also argue that Jews tend to be more concerned about certain social issues, such as providing educational opportunities, than are other people. I will leave it to others to argue whether there is a sense of a "larger class of persons" which Jewish Senators and Congressmen are better able to represent.[4]

However, if one accepts the argument that there is a need for descriptive representation, one should acknowledge that it is often accompanied by a claim that a certain group is not represented by members of that group in proportion to their number.[5] One cannot make that claim for Jews. Depending on how one counts, Jews represent between 1.5% and 2% of the American population.[6] Even with their diminished numbers in the 113th Congress, Jews hold about 5% of the seats in the House of Representatives and 9% of the Senate seats, down from previous highs but still well above expectation for mathematically proportional representation.

The second line of reasoning, regarding why this subject is important, relates to identity-politics. More particularly, how do Jews self-identify and how are Jews identified by others involved in the electoral process? Jews were proud when Joe Lieberman was tapped as Al Gore's running mate in 2000. But some were also nervous, fearing that his nomination would foment anti-Semitism or that he would be blamed if Gore lost because the Lieberman candidacy dragged Gore down. Jewish public opinion reflected relief and pride when Lieberman's candidacy was evaluated favorably by the general, voting population, when pundits concluded that as vice presidential candidate, Lieberman contributed positively to the campaign's successes and was not a significant, contributing factor in its failures, and that, in the final analysis, Gore's loss should be blamed more on other factors rather than on the fact that Lieberman was Jewish.

In terms of this study, the question related to identity-politics turns on whether Jews vote for Jews because they are Jews and, on the other side of the coin, whether non-Jews vote against Jews because they are Jews. Those types of voting decisions are the theoretical assumption behind the creation of majority-minority districts. The argument posits that not only can a member of a group represent other members of that group more effectively, but also voters not in that group will not support members of the group, precisely because of the candidate's group-identification. With these points established, let us turn to an examination of the recent electoral history of Jews running for the US House of Representatives, the United States Senate and State Governor and what this can reveal to us.

## JEWS IN THE UNITED STATES HOUSE OF REPRESENTATIVES

Including the twenty-two currently in office, 125 Jews have served in the United States House of Representatives since the end of the Second World War. As shown in Figure 1, the number of Jews in the House hovered around ten until the Kennedy administration, reached twenty for the first time in the 94th Congress, elected in 1974, and peaked at thirty-four in the 102nd Congress, elected in 1990. The number has fluctuated since that time, dropping to twenty-three in the 106th Congress (1998 election), rising back to thirty-two with the election of the 111th Congress in 2008, and falling to the lowest point since the 96th Congress, elected in 1978, with the most recent election, to the 113th Congress.

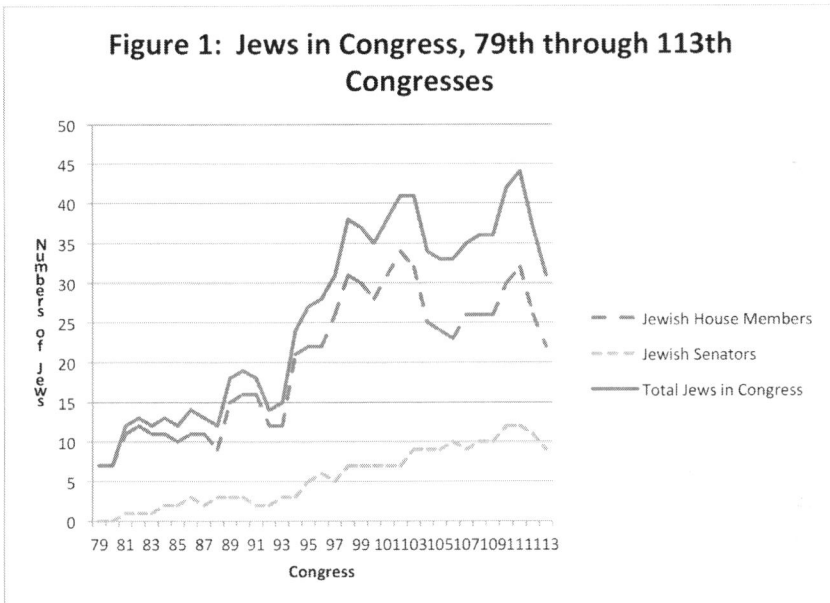

Figure 1:  Jews in Congress, 79th through 113th Congresses

One might conclude from this review that the recent line trends to the negative and that the future of Jews in Congress does not look too bright. But a more nuanced analysis leads to a different conclusion.

Trend-lines are indeed important. At the beginning of our period of study, Jews by-and-large were elected from districts with large Jewish populations.[7] In half of the first ten Congresses examined, at least two-thirds of the Jewish Members of Congress came from districts within the five boroughs of New York City. Only three of the Members elected in that period came from metropolitan areas with fewer than 250,000 Jews; that is, most came from areas with large Jewish populations.

However, Figures 2 and 3 show that this pattern was not maintained. Figure 2 charts the number of House districts in each Congress in which Jewish Members were elected from districts with metropolitan area Jewish populations under 100,000, between 100,000 and 250,000, and over 250,000. Figure 3 presents these numbers as a percentage of the total Jewish membership of the House.

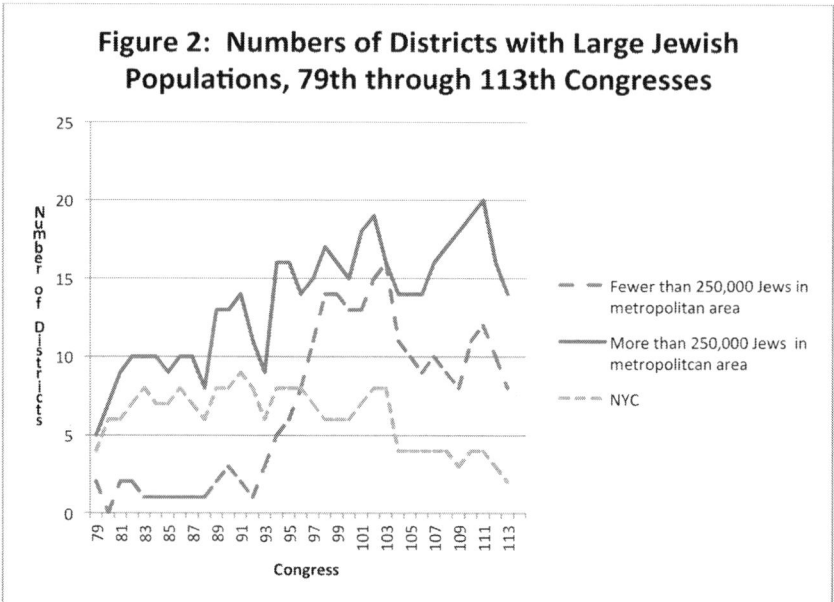

Figure 2:  Numbers of Districts with Large Jewish Populations, 79th through 113th Congresses

## Figure 3:  Percentage of Jewish Congressmen from Districts with Large Jewish Populations, 79th through 113th Congress

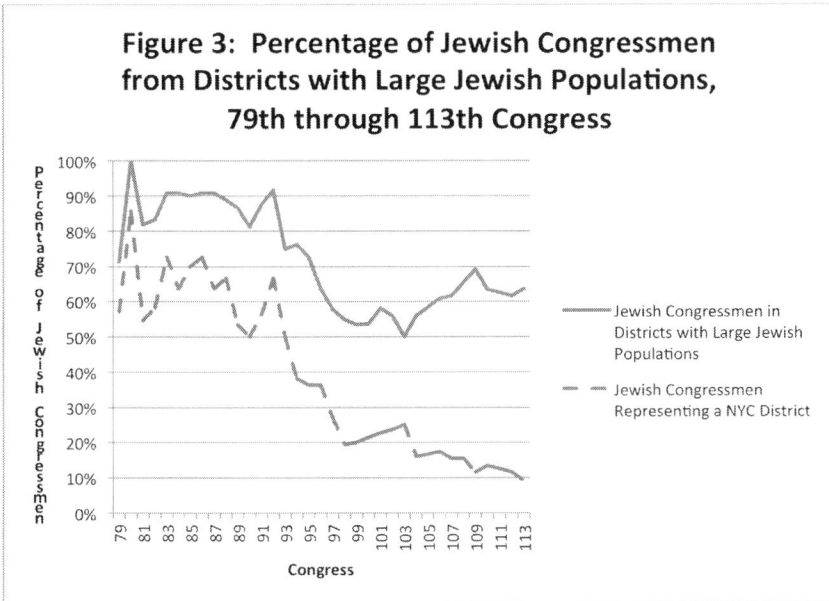

The number of Members from districts without large Jewish communities began to rise with the election of 1974, to the 94th Congress; the number began a sharp decline with the election of the 104th Congress, in 1994. From Figure 3 we can extrapolate two factors. First, the percentage of Jewish Members from districts with large Jewish communities has declined over the period of our study. Even more striking is the sharp decline in the percentage (and number) of Jewish Members from New York City. Whereas once the image of Jews in Congress was that of Emanuel ("Manny") Celler (D-NY) and Abraham ("Abe") Multer (D-NY) and others out of the New York City political machines, today Jerrold Nadler (D-NY) and Eliot Engel (D-NY) are the only Jews representing New York City districts; the more typical Jewish Member might be Steven Israel (D-NY) from suburban Long Island, Deborah ("Debbie") Wasserman-Schultz (D-FL) from south Florida, or Stephen Cohen (D-TN) from Nashville, Tennessee.

These observations lead to a number of conclusions, ones which might appear obvious to veteran observers of Congressional elections but which are less clear to those concerned principally with Jewish representation. The first is a consequence of political geography. Americans are a mobile lot, and as population densities shift, Congressional districts are reapportioned, accordingly.

After World War II, forty-five Congressmen represented New York State in the House of Representatives, about half of those from metropolitan New

York City; by 2012, that number had declined to twenty-seven, with urban-dominated districts fewer than half of the state's delegation. Toward the opposite extreme, California's delegation has grown from twenty-three to fifty-three; Florida's from six to twenty-seven. Some areas that had traditionally been represented by Jews—and which remained centers of Jewish population—lost representation in Congress because of population shifts.

At the same time, Jews were moving into new areas, and also expanding into other areas. Thus, it is not surprising that four of the 113th Congress' Jewish Members are from Florida (three from south Florida) and four are from California (three from the Los Angeles area). Emerging Jewish communities are often represented by Jews in the same way as traditional Jewish communities had been a generation ago.

According to David Paul's study of Congressional districts, as they existed in 2006 (and generally were in place for all elections between 2002 and 2010), among the top thirty districts in terms of Jewish population were eight districts that were at least partially made up of parts of New York City, but two of those were majority-minority districts, districts in which a majority of the population was either African-American or Hispanic-American. Four of those eight districts were represented by Jews. Five of those thirty districts were in California, three represented by Jews. Four were in Florida, three represented by Jews. The other thirteen districts with most Jews in them—found typically in suburbs or larger cities including Boston, New York, Philadelphia, Baltimore, and Chicago—elected five Jews and eight non-Jews to the House.

It is important to note, however, that in none of these districts did Jews comprise 50% of the population (the largest was actually under 40% in Florida's 19th Congressional District [parts of Palm Beach and Broward Counties], represented at the time by Robert Wexler [D-FL]); in only four of them, all represented by Jews, did Jews count for even a quarter of the population; and in those near the bottom of the top thirty, Jews made up less than 10% of the population.

The conclusion is that Jewish Representatives in these areas with prominent Jewish communities were elected, by-and-large, by non-Jews. Of course, that is even more true of the roughly dozen members who have been elected on average over the last thirty years from districts with even smaller Jewish communities. Thus an important point to keep in mind, when one looks at the trend-line for Jews elected to Congress, is that they have been elected from different regions of the country. Moreover, the changing patterns have reflected shifts in population nationally (thereby affecting apportionment among the states) and of Jews, in particular, and that to a large extent these members—both when the number of Jews in Congress has risen and when it has been falling—have been elected largely by non-Jewish electorates.

One may therefore make a strong case that the willingness of non-Jewish citizens to be represented by Jews, and their inclination not to think of Jews as "others," is an important factor in the dramatic increase in the number of Jews elected to Congress over the last three decades. However, the decline in the number of Jews in Congress in the most recent election (and at other periods in our recent history) has another—and far simpler—explanation.

Of the 125 Jews who have served in the United States House of Representatives since World War II, 108 have been Democrats, fifteen Republicans.[8] The second factor that has led to the decrease in the number of Jews serving in the House is related directly to the fate of the Democratic Party. As Figure 1 reveals, during two periods the number of Jewish Members of Congress dropped precipitously—following the 1994 election and the 2010 election. In both of those elections, the Democrats lost more than fifty seats, about one in every five Democratic Members. Prior to the 1994 election, there were twenty-seven Jewish Democrats, four Jewish Republicans, and one Jewish Independent. After the election, the numbers were twenty, four and one, respectively. Prior to the 2010 election, thirty-one Jewish Democrats were serving in the House, along with one Jewish Republican; after the election, the number of Jewish Democrats was reduced to twenty-five. Again, Jews lost because they were Democrats, running in a year in which many other Democrats also lost.

Another way to look at this history is to examine a few case-studies of Jews in Congress. Of course, no Member's career can be thought of as typical of all Members of Congress, but some clear patterns emerge. One such pattern is—and, as already mentioned, this is a common characteristic applicable to Representatives across the board—that a Congressman, once elected from a heavily Jewish district, tends to remain in that seat for a long period of time. Thus, Henry Waxman (D-CA) was elected from his Los Angeles area district in 1975 and has remained in Congress ever since, rarely facing serious competition.[9] Waxman is now the longest serving Jewish Member of Congress. Often Jewish Members from heavily Jewish districts came to office succeeding another Jewish Member; and it is not unusual for them to be succeeded by another Jewish Member. For example, Jerry Nadler has represented lower Manhattan since 1992; he was preceded in office by Theodore Weiss (D-NY), who was, in turn, preceded by Bella Abzug (D-NY).

Another pattern concerns a Jewish Member who has been elected from an area without a large Jewish population—and, as is typically the case for an incumbent, remains in the House for a considerable period of time. Martin Frost (D-TX) represented the Dallas area from 1979 until 2005, rising to be the third ranking Democrat in the House. The Jewish population of Dallas more than doubled during his time in the House; when he was first elected, the Jewish population of the entire metropolitan Dallas area was estimated to be less than 25,000. Daniel Glickman (D-KS) from Wichita, Kansas, and Samuel Gejdenson (D-CT) from New London, Connecticut also fit this pattern, as do many others. Generally, these Members are the first Jewish Members from their districts; and most often, when they lose their seats, they are replaced by non-Jews.

A third pattern concerns a Jewish Member, elected from an area without a large Jewish population, who remains in the House for only a short period of time and then is replaced by a non-Jew. For example, John Krebs (D-CA) was elected to the House from Fresno, California, in 1974; the first foreign-born citizen to be elected to Congress from California, Krebs was defeated four years later by Charles Pashayan, Jr. (R-CA). Similarly, Steve Kagen (D-WI) from Appleton, Wisconsin, one of the few physicians ever elected to the House, won his seat in 2006, was re-elected in 2008, but then was defeated in 2010, by Reid Ribble (R-WI).

Losing after short terms in the House is a fate shared by some elected from areas with larger Jewish populations. Marjorie Margolies-Mezvinsky (D-PA) from suburban Philadelphia rode into office on the Democratic tide that accompanied Bill Clinton's election in 1992, narrowly beating Jon Fox (R-PA). Fox, who is also Jewish, reminded voters of Margolies-Mezvinsky's decisive and highly visible vote for raising taxes and turned the tables on her in 1994. Two years later Fox survived a re-election battle by fewer than one hundred votes; and in 1996, after surviving a hard-fought primary, he lost a rematch to Joseph Hoeffel (D-PA).

The common points that may be seen among all of these patterns is that they share elements that are characteristic for the careers of many other, non-Jewish Members of Congress. Some Members serve a long time. Why do they leave? They retire because they have served long enough (Sidney Yates [D-IL], Benjamin Gilman [R-NY]) or because the political landscape might be changing—say, after redistricting—and they are not interested in introducing themselves to new voters all over again (Barney Frank). They are defeated because of redistricting (Howard Berman) or because the national political climate has turned against them (Martin Frost). Occasionally they leave to run for other office (Bernie Sanders, Charles Schumer [D-NY]) or to accept another position (Abner Mikva [D-IL], Daniel Glickman). The short-termers almost always leave involuntarily, because the voters chose to send someone else in their place.

In the early period covered by this study, from the end of World War II until roughly the Kennedy years, only four Jews were elected who were not from areas with large Jewish populations. One of those, labor leader Leonard Irving (D-MO) from Jefferson City, Missouri, served only two terms. The other three were elected from cities with small, but growing Jewish populations, such as Samuel Friedel (D-MD) from Baltimore. Of the eleven Jews serving at the end of the 1950s, six succeeded Jews in their seats and two were the first Members elected from newly created districts. Though they left Congress at various times, all eleven of these Members were succeeded by Jews. That is pretty good evidence that these Jews represented districts in which Jews were a known and influential quantity.

But increasingly in the last half century, the electoral history of Jews in the House of Representatives has been pretty similar to the history of other Democrats in the House of Representatives. Some serve constituencies in which Jews are prominent; others do not. Anecdotally, I believe that the same can be said of Irish-Americans, Italian-Americans, and those of other ethnic backgrounds. It is difficult to prove this claim empirically, however, because it is easier to know who is a Jew than it is to know who to count as an Italian-American or an Irish-American. The Jews whose electoral history I have analyzed are all self-identified Jews. For most of them, their Jewishness is a prominent characteristic.

I would have thought the same would hold true of Irish-Americans and Italian-Americans—and that, therefore, parallel studies could be done. But that has turned out not to be the case. None of the groups that list Irish-American or Italian-American Members of Congress have historical records. Further, while Jews sometimes dance on the head of a pin when they go about defining who is Jewish and who is not, other ethnic groups tend to err on the side of inclusiveness. The National Italian-American Foundation, for instance, lists among the Italian-American Members of Congress Representatives Michael Doyle (D-PA), Kevin McCarthy (R-CA), and Timothy Ryan (D-OH). Each of these men is of Italian-American heritage; but none is principally known as Italian-American. The various lists of Irish-American politicians are even more inclusive. Thus, it is hard to know how to go beyond conventional wisdom—

and the conventional wisdom is that some ethnic Members represent districts in which their ethnic group is prominent and some do not. It is also true that districts that are dominated by one ethnic group tend to be represented by a group member. According to David Paul's study of Congressional district populations, far more districts have concentrations of Irish-Americans and Italian-Americans (over 10%) than is the case with Jews; but roughly the same number of districts have 25% who are members of either of these groups, and neither has a majority in any district.[10]

Interestingly, African-American and Hispanic-American Members of Congress can be differentiated from Jews and these other groups based on this ethnic factor. First, of course, both because of residential patterns and because of purposeful redistricting, majority African-American and majority Hispanic-American districts have been created.[11] In the 112th Congress, there were twenty-seven districts with African-American majorities, and twenty-six of them were represented by African-Americans. Seventeen African-Americans from non-African-American majority districts served in that Congress; fifteen of them from districts that were at least 20% African-American, a number from districts with significant Hispanic-American populations. Thirty districts had Hispanic-American majorities in the 112th Congress; twenty-four were represented by Hispanic-American Members of Congress; only four Hispanic-Americans in the 112th did not represent majority Hispanic-American districts. In terms of electability, it seems that the premise behind the creation of majority-minority districts held true; non-minority voters are far less likely to elect minority Congressman than are non-Jewish voters (or non-Italian-American or non-Irish-American voters) inclined to elect Jewish Congressmen (or Congressmen from these other ethnic groups).

What about the other end of a career? Jewish Congressmen retire, are defeated, or seek other office for pretty much the same reasons as is the case for other Members of Congress, who retire, seek higher office, or are defeated. They do so because of age, because of changes in the political climate, or scandal. They are defeated because of partisan waves going against their party or because they have been redistricted into a less favorable seat. They seek higher office because the opportunity presents itself. They accept national, appointive office because the President asks them to serve.[12]

My conclusion is that Jewish Members of Congress are not very different—in terms of winning office, the districts they represent, and how and when they leave office—than other Members of Congress. As the vast majority of the Jewish Representatives have been Democrats, in the last half century their political fate has largely mirrored that of the Democratic Party. The change from Jews serving as Jews largely from Jewish districts to Jews serving as politicians as all others do—some from Jewish districts and some not—started in the 1960s and has accelerated during the last two decades. In my view the best interpretation of what has happened to Jewish representation in the House in the last two cycles has much more to do with 2010 being a bad year for Democrats and the 2012 redistricting reflecting changing residential patterns that have hurt a number of Jewish Congressmen than it does with any factor related to a given Representative's religion.

## JEWS IN THE SENATE AND IN GOVERNORS' MANSIONS
The conclusion I have drawn about electoral patterns related to Jews in the House of Representatives is buttressed by the experience of Jews serving in the Senate and serving as Governors. Though the numbers involved in both cases are so small as to make generalizations questionable, nonetheless the patterns revealed remain important.

*Governors.* Thirteen Jews from eleven different states have served as Governor of their home states since the end of World War Two. As noted in Table 1, twelve of those Governors were elected; one, Samuel Shapiro (D-IL), was elected Lieutenant Governor, succeeded to the governorship when his predecessor resigned, and then ran unsuccessfully for Governor in his own right.

**TABLE 1**
**Jewish Governors, 1945–2013**

| Name | State | Party | Years of Service |
|------|-------|-------|------------------|
| Ernest H. Gruening | Alaska | D | 1939–1953 |
| Abraham Ribicoff | Connecticut | D | 1955–1961 |
| Samuel H. Shapiro* | Illinois | D | 1968–1969 |
| Frank Licht | Rhode Island | D | 1969–1973 |
| Marvin Mandel** | Maryland | D | 1969–1979 |
| Milton J. Shapp | Pennsylvania | D | 1971–1979 |
| Madeline M. Kunin | Vermont | D | 1985–1991 |
| Neil Goldschmidt | Oregon | D | 1987–1991 |
| Bruce G. Sundlun | Rhode Island | D | 1991–1995 |
| Linda Lingle | Hawaii | R | 2002–2010 |
| Edward Rendell | Pennsylvania | D | 2003–2011 |
| Eliot Spitzer*** | New York | D | 2007–2008 |
| Jack Markell | Delaware | D | 2009– |

* Elected as Lieutenant Governor in 1960 and 1964; succeeded to Governorship with the resignation of Otto Kerner in 1968; lost bid for election in his own right in 1968.
** In June 1977 after conviction on a mail fraud charge (later overturned) Mandell took a leave from the Governorship, requesting that Lieutenant Governor Blair Lee served as Acting Governor.
*** Resigned in March 2008 as a result of a scandal involving his personal behavior.

What insights can we draw from the careers of these Governors? First, as noted in our discussion of House Members, some come from states with large Jewish populations and others come from states with relatively few Jews.[13] There was certainly an up-tick in Jews elected to Governors' mansions after the Kennedy and Johnson Administrations, but there were also two periods of time—between the elections of 1978 and 1984 and between those of 1992 and 2002—when no Jews served as State Governor. Four of the Jews elected as Governor in the last thirty years came from states in which no city has a prominent Jewish population.

How did these individuals rise to the governorships of their respective states?—pretty much the same way as other Governors reached their posts. Many served in state legislatures; others were elected as either Lieutenant Governor or Attorney General in statewide elections or served as mayor of a large city. That is to say, the norm for these Jewish Governors, as it is for other Governors, is to work their way up through the political ranks. Only one,

Milton Shapp (D-PA), self-financed a gubernatorial campaign more or less out of the blue. And Shapp lost in his first effort. His loss, however, was not unusual. Two others lost in their first race for the State House; two also lost in bids for re-election. All save one of the Jewish Governors have been Democrats; in recent years all of the Jewish Governors, including Linda Lingle (R-HI), the only Republican on this list, won in states that are solidly in support of Democrats.

Two of the Governors (Gruening [D-AK] and Ribicoff [D-CT]) later served in the United States Senate (and Ribicoff is the only Jewish Governor who had previously served in the US House). One had served in a President's Cabinet (Goldschmidt [D-OR]); one resigned to accept a Cabinet post (Ribicoff); and one succeeded to the governorship when his predecessor accepted a Presidential appointment to the federal appeals court (Shapiro). Madeline Kunin (D-VT), in addition to having been appointed to a sub-Cabinet position, was appointed United States Ambassador to Switzerland; Edward Rendell (D-PA) became chairman of the Democratic National Committee.

The Jews who served as State Governors during the period, as a group, look very much like any other subset of successful (particularly Democratic) politicians during this time period. While their religion may have had an impact on some of their policy positions and the emphases they placed on certain policies while in office, it is difficult to argue that their religion was a determining factor in their electoral success.

***United States Senators.*** As the table in Figure 1 indicates, the number of Jewish Senators initially stayed quite low and then made jumps at approximately the same times that the line for Jewish Representatives moved upward. As there are only one hundred Senators, compared to 435 Congressmen, a jump in Jewish Senate membership of a given number of Senators represents more than four times a similar jump in House membership. Had the figure been constructed showing percentage of Jews in each body, the line for Jewish Senators would have jumped more precipitously. However, because Senators are elected for six-year terms, the distinct drops on the House side have not been exactly mirrored on the Senate side. A differentiating factor concerns whether or not a particular Jewish seat was contested in a bad year for Democrats. Of course, reapportionment and the shifting residential patterns, noted above in the discussion of the House of Representatives, do not impact Senate seats held by a given state, which remain constant at two.

A number of other factors, regarding Jews in the Senate merit attention. First, while most Jewish Senators in the last two decades have been Democrats, this preponderance of Democratic Jewish Senators was not always in evidence.

For more than two decades after the 1956 election, when Jacob Javits (R-NY) was elected as a Republican Senator from New York, the Jewish Senate "caucus" never had more than three members—and one of them was always Republican. From the election of 1978 through the election of 1990, at least two of the Jews in the Senate were Republicans (first Javits and Rudolph Boschwitz [R] of Minnesota in the 96th Congress; then Boschwitz, and Warren Rudman [R] of New Hampshire and Arlen Specter [R, later D] of Pennsylvania in the 97th Congress; then Boschwitz, Rudman, Specter, and Jacob "Chic" Hecht [R] of Nevada for the 98th through 100th Congresses; then Hecht did not return for the 101st, Boschwitz was replaced by Paul Wellstone [D-MN], a Jewish Democrat for the 102nd; and Rudman did not return for the 103rd). Since the 103rd Congress convened in 1993, at least nine Jews have been present at the beginning of each new Congress; at least eight of whom have been Democrats. There were two Jewish Republican Senators in the 110th Congress—Specter and Norman Coleman of Minnesota. Coleman lost his reelection bid and Specter switched to the Democratic Party during the 111th Congress. As no Jewish Republicans were serving in the Senate during the recent Republican gains, any Jewish losses had to be from Democratic seats. Thus, the recent drop in Jewish membership (which still leaves nine Jewish Senators, a far larger percentage of the Senate than the Jewish proportion of the population) should be attributed to partisan losses, not to the religion of the losing candidates.

Of the twenty-six post-World War II Jewish Senators, listed in Table 2, all save three (Richard Stone [D-FL], Hecht, and Coleman) served more than one term. Twelve of the remaining eighteen, who have finished their second term, served more than two full terms. These men and women came to the Senate through quite traditional paths. Seven had served in the House of Representatives, the single most common path to the Senate; others had been elected to office statewide, most frequently Attorney General, but also Governor in smaller states. While most would be deemed career politicians, at least three self-financed their campaigns after successful business careers (Howard Metzenbaum [D-OH], Frank Lautenberg [D-NJ], and Kohl) and one (Alan ["Al"] Franken [D-MN]) used the name-recognition he had obtained as a comedian to become a front-line candidate, when he had to campaign in his own right on the issues.

| TABLE 2 Jewish United States Senators, 1945–2013 | | | |
|---|---|---|---|
| **Senator** | **Party** | **State** | **Years in Senate** |
| Herbert Lehman | D | NY | 1949–1957 |
| Richard Neuberger | D | OR | 1955–1960 |
| Jacobs Javits | R | NY | 1957–1981 |
| Ernest Gruening | D | AK | 1959–1969 |
| Abraham Ribicoff | D | CT | 1963–1981 |
| Howard Metzenbaum | D | OH | 1974; 1976–1995* |
| Richard Stone | D | FL | 1975–1980 |
| Edward Zorinsky | D | NE | 1976–1987** |
| Rudolph Boschwitz | R | MN | 1978–1991*** |
| Warren Rudman | R | NH | 1980–1993**** |
| Arlen Specter | R | PA | 1981–2011 |
| Frank Lautenberg | D | NJ | 1982–2001; 2003–***** |
| Chic Hecht | R | NV | 1983–1989 |
| Herbert Kohl | D | WI | 1989–2013 |
| Joseph Lieberman | D | CT | 1989–2013 |
| Paul Wellstone | D | MN | 1991–2002 |
| Diane Feinstein | D | CA | 1992–****** |
| Barbara Boxer | D | CA | 1993– |
| Russell Feingold | D | WI | 1993–2011 |
| Ronald Wyman | D | OR | 1996–******* |
| Charles Schumer | D | NY | 1999– |
| Norm Coleman | R | MN | 2003–2009 |
| Benjamin Cardin | D | MD | 2007– |
| Bernie Sanders | I | VT | 2007– |
| Al Franken | D | MN | 2009– |
| Richard Blumenthal | D | CT | 2011– |

\* Metzenbaum was elected in 1976 and took office at the end of that year, but did not really serve in the 94th Congress.

\*\* Zorinsky was elected in 1976 and took office at the end of that year, but did not really serve in the 94th Congress; he died in March, 1987, serving only three months in the 100th Congress.

\*\*\* Boschwitz was elected in 1978 and took office at the end of that year, but did not really serve in the 95th Congress.

\*\*\*\* Rudman was elected in 1980 and took office at the end of that year, but did not really serve in the 96th Congress.

\*\*\*\*\* Lautenberg was elected in 1982 and took office at the end of that year, but did not really serve in the 97th Congress

\*\*\*\*\*\* Feinstein was elected in 1992 and took office at the end of that year, but did not really serve in the 102nd Congress.

\*\*\*\*\*\*\* Wyden is counted as a member of the 104th Congress as he was elected in January of that year.

Only four of the Jewish Senators succeeded Jewish Senators—one in New York, which certainly is not surprising, but the other three in Minnesota (certainly not thought to be a state with traditional Jewish prominence), where the seat went from Boschwitz to Wellstone to Coleman to Franken. These twenty-six Senators represented sixteen different states; as noted, four were from Minnesota, three each were from New York and Connecticut, and two from California, Oregon, and Wisconsin. Sixteen of these Senators were the first Jews to represent their state in the United States Senate. And it is striking that during this period Jews represented not only New York, New Jersey, Pennsylvania, California and Florida, but also Minnesota, Wisconsin, Alaska, Nebraska, New Hampshire and Vermont.

More than a third of the Jewish Senators from this period are still serving. The career paths of those who have left the Senate have also been instructive. Some, like Javits and Specter, simply stayed too long; the voters told them it was past time to go, after distinguished careers. Others like Boschwitz and Coleman, Hecht and Russell Feingold (D-WI), lost because the politics of the time went against their party. Some quit when it was time to quit, as Frank Lautenberg announced his intention to do before he died.

The lesson derived from considering Jews serving in the United States Senate cements the conclusion hinted at by examining House careers and reinforced by the analysis of Jewish Governors. Jewish politicians are now so well assimilated into the American body politic that, in seeking elective office at the national level and pursuing their careers as national figures, they have had successes or failures in ways very similar to non-Jews. Non-Jewish voters evaluate Jewish candidates as they do other candidates, at times positively and at times negatively, but rarely with much emphasis placed upon their religion.

## CONCLUSION

The premise for this brief study has been to consider whether Jews, who follows politics closely, should be concerned because, overall, Jewish representation in the House and Senate has declined in the last two election cycles and has reached a point lower than at any time in the last three decades. I would contend that a broader perspective is needed.

Let us not look back just at the last thirty years but instead go back to the end of the Second World War. I think Jews should be mindful of the length of service and the growing authority that was achieved, for example, by Adolph Sabath (D-IL), Sol Bloom (D-NY), and Manny Celler within the House of Representatives. Jews also have a right to be proud of Senators of the caliber of Herbert Lehman and Jacob Javits. It is not so much that they were only Jews representing New York or Chicago, but rather they are rightly seen as Jews who were players on the national stage. By the same token, Jews can take particular pride in the career of Abe Ribicoff, a Governor, a Cabinet officer, a United States Senator, and a leader not only within his party, but on the national stage. Very few political leaders on the national scene have been Jewish; Jews should take note of and express pride in those who have made this country a better place.

Still, as more Jews have been elected to positions of national power, the novelty of this considerable achievement has worn off. Over time, for Jewish voters and Jewish politicians, identity-politics, while still somewhat in play, has been less in evidence. That a candidate is Jewish has become less a part of the campaign message for those running for office and less a part of the decision matrix for those deciding for whom to vote. Arguably, a greater prominence for identity-politics reentered the picture with the Vice Presidential nomination of Joe Lieberman, making him potentially the proverbial "one heartbeat away" from the Presidency. Still, because he performed so well, his religion was not seen as the factor determining whether either Jews or non-Jews supported him. Jews could now be viewed as electable to *any* national office. Lieberman's candidacy demonstrated this not only to party leaders, but also to his fellow Jews, who had feared that Lieberman's candidacy would be detrimental to, rather than as a harbinger for, future Jewish candidacies.

The question then becomes whether anything has happened in the decade or so since Lieberman's candidacy to reverse this near half-century long movement toward acceptance of Jewish politicians as assimilated Americans, after the manner of Italian-Americans, Irish-Americans, and in fact all Catholic-Americans, who have been accepted for a somewhat longer period of time.

Perhaps the most apt comparison is to African-American politicians. When Barack Obama was elected as the first African-American President in 2008, observers commented that the last barrier for African-Americans had been broken. But had it? Since Reconstruction only three African-Americans have been elected to the United States Senate (Edward Brooke [R] of Massachusetts, Carol Moseley-Braun [D] of Illinois, and Obama[14]). Only two have been elected as their state's Governor—Douglas Wilder (D) in

Virginia and Deval Patrick (D), the current Governor of the Commonwealth of Massachusetts; one other, David Paterson (D) of New York, succeeded to the Governorship upon the resignation of his predecessor, Eliot Spitzer (D); but Paterson withdrew from the Democratic Primary for Governor in February before the 2010 election. In most recent Congresses about forty African-Americans have served in the House. Of course, there are roughly six times as many African American in the United States as Jews; that there are twice as many in Congress is therefore hardly surprising. As noted above, however, interpretation of this number must include acknowledgement that states have been creating majority-minority districts for more than twenty years and that most of the African-Americans in Congress (though clearly not all) come from such districts. Without majority-minority districts, a different picture would emerge. While no Jew has received a major party nomination for President, Jewish politicians generally are more likely to be accepted by majority non-Jewish districts and states (all states and all districts are non-Jewish majority) than is the case for African-Americans.

The same conclusion could be drawn for Hispanic-Americans, although Hispanic Americans have been more successful at winning statewide office than has been the case for African-Americans. Seven Hispanic Americans have been elected as State Governor in recent years (four in New Mexico, one each in Arizona, Florida, and Nevada), and eight Hispanic-Americans have been elected to the United States Senate. All but one, and virtually all of the Hispanic-Americans in the House, have been elected from areas with large Hispanic-American populations. These minority populations, protected by the provisions of the Voting Rights Act and Supreme Court decisions that seek to redress discriminatory, unequal treatment, have not been assimilated into American politics as readily as have Jews.

In the final analysis, this story is one that is typical of American politics. Jews have chosen to go into politics for a variety of reasons. They have chosen the Democratic Party, for the most part, also for a variety of reasons (as discussed by Eric Uslaner elsewhere in this volume). Their fortunes have increased as they have been accepted as effective political players; their degree of success and failure has waxed and waned with the ups and downs of the party with which they have mostly chosen to associate. But as time has progressed, their religious and ethnic affiliation has receded from the foreground into the background. In sum: Jews who run for national office today, are predominantly perceived in the public consciousness as politicians, who also happen to be Jewish rather than the other way around.

## Notes

1.  For a scholarly review of identity politics as a concept, see Bernstein and Taylor.

2.  Vermont is the only state with a population so small that it is assigned a single Representative in the House and which has ever elected a Jew to statewide office. Vermont elected Bernard ("Bernie") Sanders first to the House (1991–2007) and then to the Senate since that time. Sanders was elected to both offices as an Independent.

3.  See, as examples, Chambers and Burnham; and Sundquist, as scholarly works that describe the 1932 election as one leading to realignments of American electoral coalitions.

4.  On this subject see Greenberg and Wald. See also, on the legislative activity of Jews in Congress, McNeely and Tolchin.

5.  This argument lies behind the creation of majority-minority districts permitted under the Voting Rights Act amendments of 1982 and ruled constitutional by the Supreme Court (with caveats) in various cases. See, Grofman, Handley and Niemi.

6.  Many sources list the population of Jews in America, all differing slightly. See, as an example, "Vital Statistics."

7.  An accurate consideration of how many Jews live in Congressional districts is fraught with difficulty. The United States Census produces data at the Congressional-District level. However, the Census Bureau is specifically prohibited from asking questions about religion. The best data for the last two election cycles (i.e., the districts drawn after 1990 and 2000 censuses) are available at Paul. The Jewish population in Congressional Districts for years prior to those analyzed by Paul was estimated on a very rough, three-point scale. District lines were not used; rather, districts were rated by whether they were in a metropolitan area with fewer than 100,000 Jews, between 100,000 and a quarter of a million Jews, or more than 250,000 Jews. This analysis was further complicated by incumbent advantage in Congressional elections. For the vast majority of the elections examined, more than 90% of the incumbents who sought re-election were re-elected. Thus, once a Jewish Member is elected to the House, barring a change in his district after the decennial census and subsequent redistricting (not an inconsequential *caveat*), that Member is likely to be re-elected. His or her religion and the Jewishness of the district would then tend to be a much less important factor. For that reason, in the analysis that follows I used estimates of the Jewish population of the metropolitan area presented in "Roster K: Concentration of Jewish Population, 1800-2000," where the methodology of deriving these estimates is discussed, for the first election of each Jewish Congressman, but I did not update the population estimate for subsequent re-elections.

8. Leo Isaacson (NY) represented the American-Labor Party in the 80th Congress; Bernie Sanders (VT) was elected to the House as an Independent from the 102nd through the 109th Congresses and to the Senate, thereafter, also as an Independent.

9. In Waxman's case—and in many others in this study—the district number changed and the district boundaries changed significantly during the period of the study. I have chosen to follow particular Congressmen, not their district numbers. It is very rare for a Congressman to move from one district to a totally different district, though often, after redistricting, many Members must decide in which new district, containing elements of their old district, they will run.

10. See Paul's detailed description of his data sources.

11. Hawaii 1 is the only majority Asian-American district.

12. African-American and Hispanic-American Congressmen seem to follow the same patterns as others in regard to leaving the House.

13. In contrast to the history of elections to the House, however, none of the Jews elected Governor before the formation of the New Deal Coalition in 1932 came from states with large Jewish populations. Rather they were from Georgia, Louisiana, Idaho, Utah, New Mexico, and Oregon. The two elected in the early New Deal were from states with prominent Jewish populations, Henry Horner (D) from Illinois and Herbert Lehman (D) from New York.

14. Three others—Roland Burris (D) of Illinois, Tim Scott (R) of South Carolina, and William ("Mo") Cowan (D) from Massachusetts—were appointed to the Senate by their states' Governors, upon the resignation of a sitting Senator. None as of this writing has run for election to the seat to which he was originally appointed, though Scott is expected to do so.

## Works Cited

Bernstein, Mary and Verta Taylor. "Identity Politics." *The Wiley Blackwell Encyclopedia of Social and Political Movements.* Wiley Online Library. 14 Jan. 2013. 11 Sept. 2013 <http://onlinelibrary.wiley.com/doi/10.1002/9780470674871.wbespm104/abstract;jsessionid=37EEC43283F922752DC74BC6414FD9B7.f03t01>.

Chambers, William N. and Walter Dean Burnham. *The American Party Systems: Stages of Political Development.* New York: Oxford Univ., 1967.

Greenberg, Anna and Kenneth D. Wald. "Still Liberal after All These Years: The Contemporary Political Behavior of American Jewry." *Jews in American Politics.* Ed. L. Sandy Maisel and Ira N. Forman. Lanham, MD: Rowman & Littlefield, 2001. 161–94.

Grofman, Bernard, Lisa Handley and Richard G. Niemi. *Minority Representation and the Quest for Voting Equality.* New York: Cambridge Univ, 1992.

Mansbridge, Jane. "Should Blacks Represent Blacks and Women Represent Women? A Contingent 'Yes.'" *The Journal of Politics* 61.3 (August, 1999): 628–57.

McNeely, Connie L. and Susan J. Tolchin. "On the Hill: Jews in the United States Congress." *Jews in American Politics.* Ed. L. Sandy Maisel and Ira N. Forman. Lanham, MD: Rowman & Littlefield, 2001. 49–64.

Paul, David M. "Jewish Population Survey of Congressional Districts: 2000 and 2006." *Berman Jewish Databank.* Mandell Berman Institute—North American Jewish Data Bank at the University of Connecticut. 20 March 2013 <http://www.jewishdatabank.org/study.asp?sid=90142&tp=3>.

"Roster K: Concentration of Jewish Population, 1800–2000." *Jews in American Politics.* Ed. L. Sandy Maisel and Ira N. Forman. Lanham, MD: Rowman & Littlefield, 2001. 471–74.

Sundquist, James L. *Dynamics of the Party System: Alignment and Realignment of Political Parties in the United States.* Rev. ed. Washington, DC: Brookings, 1983.

"Vital Statistics: Jewish Population in the United States, by State (1899–Present)." *Jewish Virtual Library.* 10 Sept. 2013 <http://www.jewishvirtuallibrary.org/jsource/US-Israel/usjewpop.html>.

# SECTION TWO

# "Boxes" for Israel: The Personal Journey of a Jewish Republican

*Fred Zeidman*

I t all started with packing boxes—hundreds of boxes. In 1950s Wharton, TX my parents—owners of the local clothing store— joined their contemporaries from other small Texas towns to collect and pack goods for Israel. The Jewish State was a few years younger than me, and it needed the same care and love as any young child. However, at the age of eight, I didn't have much appreciation for the overarching ideal of building a Jewish State. I was tired. I wanted to go to sleep.

My father told me that there was no more important thing that we could do than what we were doing. "We must do everything we can do to support the State of Israel," he told me. To this day, I remember his intensity.

My parents were born in America—my father fought in World War II, and we were comfortable in small-town Texas. Wharton, TX did not boast a large Jewish community, but we had strength. Living on the periphery of American Jewish life meant that my parents continuously had to reinforce our family's and our hometown's Jewish environment. It was up to them to transmit Jewish religion and values from one generation to the next –*l-dor v-dor*. They kept kosher, no easy feat when the closest kosher butcher was sixty miles away, down a two-lane highway. We had Friday night *shabbat* dinners. My parents were involved in the synagogue, the town's only one for all levels of Jewish religious worship. My father was a member of the local B'nai B'rith Lodge, and my mother was in Hadassah. And I was in Young Judea, our local Zionist youth group.

In Wharton, I learned, *kol Yisrael arevim zeh l-zeh*, that is, each Jew is responsible for one another, which is the essence of Jewish Peoplehood. I also learned to stand up for "what was right." My parents were the best examples of this. Like other Jewish families in the American South, my father balanced his Jewish observance with his family obligations to support his family back in New York, as well as myself and my mother. This sense of responsibility extended to the broader Jewish family and to a certain extent, the larger community.

My parents *lived* their Judaism. They knew that a strong State of Israel was the best guarantor of Jewish security in America and around the world. They put their deeply held religious beliefs in *tikkun olam*—social justice—to work in their deeds. My parents became civil rights pioneers in our small Texas town. There was a Black woman, Mary Lou Brock, who worked in our store as a domestic. One afternoon, my mother came to her and told her to show up the next morning in a dress. She did, and "Joe Schwartz Everything to Wear" became the first store with a Black sales woman in Wharton, TX. Needless to say, this change was not popular to most in small-town Texas, but my parents were committed to and guided by their Jewish values.

America in the 1950s and 1960s was not necessarily open for Jews. Anti-Semitism was common, and even socially acceptable. Quotas for Jewish applicants to college were not unprecedented, and typically, Jewish students were not made to feel comfortable on Texas and other southern campuses. By the time I got to college at Washington University in St. Louis, MO things had started to change . . . but slowly.

Our house in Wharton had a dual atmosphere—not unknown in American Jewish homes—of Jewish identity and political interest. In one way or another, my mother (a Roosevelt Democrat) and my father (a Goldwater Republican) created an atmosphere that developed my interest in Jewish Peoplehood, political interest, personal responsibility, and action. They were active and, as their only child, I came along for the ride.

As you can imagine, political conversations in my household were pretty lively. Yet, they were not on issues of Israel or Jewish security. Both political parties had supported Israel, and living in Wharton, TX, we looked to a strong Israel to ensure our local Jewish community's security. No, the liveliest discussions stemmed from much deeper Jewish values surrounding domestic issues: what my mother saw as the "safety net" – government programs to care for the poor, sick and weak—what my father called "the entitlement system" versus what he saw as freedom and opportunity—the ability to make it in America and give *tzedakah* to charities that took care of those less fortunate. In my eyes, the ability to earn wealth and give *tzedakah* was a better avenue for expressing these values, because it could raise the whole society—not just a part of it. Thus, I chose to be a Republican.

In June 1967, I joined my fraternity brother Howard Cohen in Chicago for the summer break. On June 6th, when the Six-Day War broke out, Howard and his parents were going to an emergency fundraiser for Israel. As a 21-year-old, I realized that it was my time to help the Jewish State survive. My philanthropy in support of Israel began that day.

Early in my married life in Houston, my wife Kay suggested that it was time for me to set this example for my own family. I met three people who became lifelong friends and who invited me to become involved in UJA's Young Leadership Cabinet. It felt right to take up the mantle of Jewish involvement; having a young family, I recognized that it was my turn to teach the next generation *l-dor v-dor*, as my parents had taught me.

One day in 1983 I received a call from Mac Sweeny, who asked me to help him in his run for a seat in Congress. After agreeing, I did the only thing I knew to do—I reached out to a Jewish organization. I called AIPAC, which let me know that Mac Sweeny was running against the most anti-Israel member of the United States Congress. Now I was energized. As my father had told me, we Jews needed to do everything that we could do to protect and build the State of Israel. These became my "boxes" for Israel. I threw myself into the Sweeny Campaign, and we won. That led to my being invited to work in support of Phil Graham's Senatorial campaign.

Then came Tom DeLay, a Texas State Legislator who sought a seat in Congress from a suburban Houston district. After he won, I took Congressman DeLay on his first trip to Israel— along with Congressmen Ted Poe and Jack Field and other elected officials. DeLay called me each year on the night of the foreign aid bill to remind me about that trip—especially the 21-year-old tank commander stationed on the Golan Heights, who personally asked Congressman DeLay to remember him and his troops, "on the front lines for democracy," facing hostile Syrian forces, whenever an Israel-related bill came up for a vote in Congress.

In the meantime, I became increasingly involved in Jewish communal organizations—Federation, the ADL, our Temple, AIPAC, and the Republican Jewish Coalition. As my children grew and became bar and bat mitzvah—the boys in Israel—our house became the nexus of Jewish values and political activism. And with each political event we hosted or campaign I joined, Israel was at the center of the conversation. Israel's security was as primary in our house as it was in my parents' home.

Another lesson I taught my children was: always be nice to people. This is really a Jewish value, to view each person as a creation of God. Just as my parents saw the potential for a better life for Mary Lou Brock, I made sure to pay special attention to everyone with whom I came in contact—from janitor, shoe shine man, bell hop, and waiter to owner and investor. Every human being is important. This attitude was particularly important in politics, because today's State Legislator's staff person may one day run a Presidential campaign.

One day in 1993 I received a call from an old buddy from my single days in Houston, who at the time was the owner of the Texas Rangers—George W. Bush. He was putting together a campaign team to run for Governor of Texas, and wanted me to join his team. I immediately said yes—and we were off and running. We talked about Israel, and his commitment was unshakable. From that point on, I conveyed George W. Bush's unwavering support for Israel to the Jewish community whenever and wherever I could.

He also had the idea of government partnering with faith-based institutions to address society's needs. Traditionally, the Jewish community believed in a high wall of separation between religion and state, since historically Jewish institutions have not been included in the definition of "religion." However, this was an opportunity to expand this definition to include "synagogue" as well as "church"—and Israel was the key. My parents' lessons once again became part of my life: a strong and secure Israel that is a steadfast American ally guarantees Jewish rights in America.

Governor Bush allowed me to join the committee that produced a White Paper on his Faith Based Initiative. Needless to say, it was not a popular document in the Jewish community. ADL's National Commission—of which I was also a member—had a heated discussion at their annual meeting about the Governor's intentions and the implications for the Jewish community. As the conversation among two hundred Jewish leaders from around the country became more heated, I spoke up. I told them to open the document and look at the names of the committee members. "You see that last name? It's mine," I said. The room quieted down, and we were able to have a more rational conversation about the Faith Based Initiatives concept.

When Governor Bush ran for and became President, my involvement became more intense and much more important. I never forgot the lesson that each person is significant—not just the investor but the busboy, or in political terms, the fundraisers and donors of a campaign, as well as the staff and the individual voters at the grassroots. It's the political equivalent of *kol Yisrael arevim zeh l-zeh.* Simultaneously, I continued to be involved with state and local races, as well as hosting a monthly gathering of young Jewish Republicans in Washington, thereby hopefully taking *l-dor v-dor* to new levels.

Thinking back on those boxes that we worked so hard to pack in 1950s Wharton, TX, I realize that every generation has its own "boxes" to pack for Israel and the Jewish People. Our responsibility is to transmit these values through personal example of involvement by creating an environment that reflects Jewish values and Peoplehood. *L-dor v-dor*, from generation to generation, as my parents demonstrated, we must *live* our Judaism, our homes must be a nexus of politics and Judaism, and we must do everything we can to support the State of Israel, because without a strong and secure Israel, our lives as Jews in America will be less secure.

# Why My Party Is the
# Best Choice for Jewish Voters

## *Matthew Brooks*

The Republican Party is the party of Abraham Lincoln and Ronald Reagan, of Jack Kemp, Max Fisher (founder of the Republican Jewish Coalition) and Eric Cantor. Their principles and the policies derived from them are the best expressions of the American ideal. Their party, my party, is the best home for all Americans, but perhaps especially for Jewish-Americans.

The Republican Party's core principles of individual freedom—economic liberty, responsibility for one's neighbors who are poor, elderly, or suffering, the vital importance of strong families and strong communities—all of these resonate deeply with Jewish voters, because they are based on Jewish values. Jewish tradition teaches that every individual has free will, that supporting those in need is a personal and communal obligation, and that the highest form of *tzedaka* (righteousness) is helping someone earn an independent living. With these ideas in mind, the Republican Party seeks to solve the problems of our day with policies that safeguard our freedoms, both personal and economic, that promote family and community, and that address problems at the nearest level (local or state) whenever possible.

Our founding fathers warned against allowing too much power to rest in one area of government. They set up a system of federal checks and balances, instituted a bicameral legislature, and put great emphasis on the role of the states. And yet time and again, there have been efforts to collect power in the hands of a few and let those few make choices for the people, distribute benefits to the people, and take resources from the people in order to do so.

If we remain true to the core principles outlined above, we can see how our economic policies should be directed. For example, by increasing freedom in economic activity, we promote growth and prosperity for all.

## ECONOMIC FREEDOM

Jack Kemp was an inspiring public servant. He was a mentor of mine, and I am proud to have worked with him. His pro-growth, pro-trade ideas came from a profound belief that free markets benefit minorities and the poor by enlarging the economic pie. He looked for ways to bring more jobs, more opportunities, and more economic freedom to people in the inner cities. His eye was always on making it easier for someone to find work and rise out of poverty or grow their business and benefit the whole community.

One way we can do that today is to remove impediments to hiring. Regulations, rising health care costs, uncertainty about taxes, and extraordinarily slow economic growth hurt small and large businesses alike and prevent them from expanding and hiring. Health care is a particularly important issue. Obamacare has already begun to raise costs, hurt job creation, limit access to care, and take away choices from doctors and patients. We need health care reforms that maintain the necessary safety net for those in need while using market forces to keep prices down. We need reforms that preserve the relationship between doctors and patients, promote more choices and more accountability in health care, and make health insurance affordable, portable, and continuous. Republicans have developed plans to do just that.

It is also imperative that we reform areas of ineffective and bloated government spending. One thing the sequester has shown is that, when there is a real will to cut back on government spending, there are ways to do so without hurting vital services. With a little flexibility and accountability, government can shed wasteful spending and focus on its proper functions. We must cut spending; our current deficits and increasing foreign-owned debt cannot continue.

## THE FIGHT FOR FREEDOM

The Founding Fathers rebelled against the tyranny of a king. Later American leaders fought against slavery, Nazism, and communism. In each generation, freedom is threatened. Our country's strength defends not only American citizens, but free people around the world. Our vigilance and willingness to fight for freedom must never waver.

Unfortunately, they have wavered in recent years, with the result that the US has been weakened in the eyes of our allies and our enemies. From Great Britain to Russia to China to Egypt, respect for the United States has fallen around the world. I am a Republican because my party stands for a principled policy that puts America's national interests first and that projects American diplomatic, economic, and if absolutely necessary, military strength to protect those interests.

Iran is a special cause for concern. The threat that a nuclear Iran poses is immense—for the United States, for our allies, and for stability in a key strategic region of the world. Time is running out, talk has failed, and it is imperative that the US be willing and able to keep every option open for preventing a nuclear Iran. Leading Democrats see diplomacy as the key to American power. Republicans know that in the face of enemies, who are sincerely and irrevocably dedicated to the destruction of our country, talk is not enough. A strong military and the will to project power are essential to our security.

Terrorism continues to be the primary tactic of one of the world's greatest threats—especially terrorism promoted by the purveyors of radical, jihadist Islam. The US must use its resources to detect, deter, prevent and punish terrorist attacks against American citizens and interests. Republicans recognize that our national security needs require the gathering of intelligence, the ability to interpret it, and the will to act on it to defend our country.

## THE REAL PRO-ISRAEL PARTY

In poll after poll, Republicans declare themselves in support of Israel in greater percentages than Democrats. They sympathize with Israel more and support Israel taking necessary action to defend the Jewish State. At the grassroots as well as in the halls of government, Israel can count on Republicans to stand in its support. Republicans view Israel as a friend who shares our values and a partner who shares many of our strategic interests and goals. We respect Israel's independence and capabilities and seek ways to work together for our common good, not to dictate a set of terms based in a certain ideological mindset.

## AN OPEN DOOR

As a people whose culture emphasizes education, critical thinking, debate, and truth-seeking, Jews are also particularly attuned to the lessons of history, to problem solving, and to the value of debunking myths. The Republican Party offers ideals and policies that look squarely at problems and look for the most effective, least intrusive, and most beneficial solutions. The Republican Party is the party that ended slavery in this country, that supported civil rights legislation, and that offers every American the security, the opportunity, and the freedom to pursue their dreams.

The traditional allegiance to Democrats in the Jewish community is fading. In four of the last five presidential election cycles, Republicans increased their share of the Jewish vote with the Jewish vote in 2012 increasing by fifty percent over 2008. Republicans continue to get more and more of the Jewish vote on the state and local levels as well. I expect that trend to continue in the future.

On a personal note, in my thirty years in politics I have always found the door of the GOP to be open to Jews. Our community is welcomed and appreciated in the party. The Republican Party has deep roots in values that are meaningful to American Jews and policies that benefit all Americans. It is time for old stereotypes and old fears about the GOP to be laid to rest.

My challenge to the Jewish community is to question the status quo, to examine the issues thoughtfully, and to make informed decisions. I firmly believe that when they step back and consider the facts, they will find that the Republican Party is the best choice for Jewish voters.

# About the Contributors

**DANIEL SCHNUR** is the Director of the Jesse M. Unruh Institute of Politics at the University of Southern California, where he works to motivate students to become active in the world of politics and encourage public officials to participate in the daily life of USC. In 2010, Schnur was appointed as Chairman of the California Fair Political Practices Commission, a position he held through that year's elections and until spring of 2011. Schnur's term as Chairman inspired him to launch Fixing California—<http://www.fixingca.com/>—an organization dedicated to campaign finance and political reform. He also served as the Co-Chairman of the Voices of Reform project, a bipartisan statewide organization devoted to making state government more responsive to the needs of California voters.

In addition to his position at USC, Schnur is an Adjunct Instructor at the University of California at Berkeley's Institute of Governmental Studies. Schnur has also held the post of Visiting Fellow at the John F. Kennedy School of Government's Institute of Politics at Harvard University and taught an advanced course in political campaign communications at George Washington University's Graduate School of Political Management. In addition, he was the founder of the Center for Campaign Leadership, a non-partisan effort to equip young people with the skills essential for professional involvement in political campaigns.

He has served as an advisor to the William & Melinda Gates Foundation, the William and Flora Hewlett Foundation, the Broad Education Foundation, the James Irvine Foundation, and the Stuart Foundation on a variety of K–12 education, college and workforce preparedness, governance and political reform efforts.

For years, Schnur was one of California's leading political and media strategists, whose record includes work on four presidential and three gubernatorial campaigns. Schnur served as the national Director of Communications for the 2000 presidential campaign of US Senator John McCain and spent five years as chief media spokesman for California Governor Pete Wilson.

Schnur's commentaries have appeared in several newspapers, including the *Los Angeles Times*, the *New York Times*, the *Washington Post*, and the *Sacramento Bee*. In addition, he has been an analyst and political commentator for CNN, MSNBC, Fox News, and National Public Radio. Schnur is a graduate of the American University in Washington, DC. He is married to Cecile Ablack, a communications and public affairs consultant, who was an Associate Dean at Yale University and Director of International

Communications and Public Affairs at the US Department of Commerce during the first Clinton Administration. See <http://dornsife.usc.edu/unruh/dan-schnur/>.

**LISA ANSELL** is Associate Director of the Casden Institute for the Study of the Jewish Role in American Life at the University of Southern California. She received her BA in French and Near East Studies from UCLA and her MA in Middle East Studies from Harvard University. She was the Chair of the World Language Department of New Community Jewish High School for five years before coming to USC in August, 2007.

**MATTHEW BROOKS** serves as Executive Director of both the Republican Jewish Coalition, an organization dedicated to enhancing ties between the Jewish community and the Republican Party, and the Jewish Policy Center, a think-tank that examines public policy from a Jewish perspective. Matt began his political career as State Chairman of the Massachusetts College Republicans while still an undergraduate at Brandeis University. Matt managed the Jack Kemp for President campaign in Massachusetts, as well as directed projects in New Hampshire and New England. Matt joined the Republican Jewish Coalition in 1988 and was appointed Executive Director of the RJC in 1990. In addition to his duties leading the RJC, Matt also serves as the organization's principal spokesman. In this role Matt has been a frequent guest on CNN, Fox News, MSNBC and has been quoted extensively in publications such as the *New York Times*, *Washington Post*, *Wall Street Journal* and other major newspapers. Matt was twice selected by *The Forward* newspaper as one of the fifty most influential Jews in America. Matt has a BA in Political Science from Brandeis University. He received an MBA from Georgetown University in March 1996.

**L. SANDY MAISEL** holds the William R. Kenan, Jr. Chair in Government at Colby College, Waterville, Maine, where he also is department chair. From 2003–012 Maisel served as founding director of Colby's Goldfarb Center for Public Affairs and Civic Engagement. Maisel is author or editor of more than twenty books, including *Jews in American Politics: An Encyclopedia* (with Ira N. Forman; Lanham, MD: Rowman & Littlefield, 2001) and *Parties and Elections in America: The Electoral Process* (with Mark D. Brewer; Lanham, MD: Rowman & Littlefield, 2011), now in its sixth edition. Most of Maisel's scholarly writing centers on congressional elections. With Walter Stone (UC-Davis) he has been co-principal investigator of the Candidate Emergence Project, a long-term examination of how individuals decide whether to run for the House of Representatives; more than a dozen refereed articles and book chapters have come from that collaboration.

**AMBASSADOR DENNIS ROSS** is counselor at The Washington Institute for Near East Policy. Prior to returning to the Institute in 2011, he served two years as special assistant to President Obama and National Security Council senior director for the

Central Region, and a year as special advisor to Secretary of State Hillary Rodham Clinton focusing on Iran. A highly skilled diplomat, Ambassador Ross was also US point man on the peace process in both the George H. W. Bush and Bill Clinton administrations. He was instrumental in assisting Israelis and Palestinians to reach the 1995 Interim Agreement, successfully brokered the 1997 Hebron Accord, facilitated the 1994 Israel-Jordan peace treaty, and intensively worked to bring Israel and Syria together. Ross is the author of several influential books and frequently publishes articles in the *New York Times*, *Washington Post*, and *Wall Street Journal*, *Foreign Policy*, and numerous other publications.

**IRA M. SHESKIN** is Professor of Geography and the Director of the Jewish Demography Project of the Sue and Leonard Miller Center for Contemporary Judaic Studies at the University of Miami. He has completed more than forty major Jewish community studies for Jewish Federations throughout the US. He served on the National Technical Advisory Committee of the Jewish Federations of North America from 1988 to 2003 which completed the 1990 and 2000–01 National Jewish Population Surveys. He also serves on the board of the North American Jewish Data Bank and is, with Arnold Dashefsky, the editor of the American Jewish Year Book.

**ERIC M. USLANER** is Professor of Government and Politics at the University of Maryland–College Park. He is Senior Research Fellow, Center for American Law and Political Science, Southwest University of Political Science and Law, Chongqing, China and Honorary Professor of Political Science, University of Aarhus, Denmark. He the author of eight books, including *The Moral Foundations of Trust* (Cambridge: Cambridge Univ., 2002); *Corruption, Inequality, and the Rule of Law: The Bulging Pocket Makes the Easy Life* (Cambridge: Cambridge Univ., 2008; paperback, 2010; Chinese translation [Beijing: Chinese Social Sciences, forthcoming 2011]; Japanese translation in progress); and *Segregation and Mistrust: Diversity, Isolation, and Social Cohesion* (Cambridge: Cambridge Univ., 2012) as well as approximately 150 articles and has received grants from the National Science Foundation and the Russell Sage and C. V. Starr Foundations. He was the Fulbright Distinguished Professor of American Political Science at the Australian National University, Canberra in 2010 and in 1981–82 was Fulbright Professor of American Studies and Political Science at the Hebrew University, Jerusalem, Israel.

**STEVEN WINDMUELLER** served as Dean of the Los Angeles campus of Hebrew Union College-Jewish Institute of Religion from 2006–10. In 2009 he was named to the Gottschalk Chair, one of only a limited number of endowed HUC faculty positions. A specialist on political issues and American Jewish affairs, Dr. Windmueller holds a doctorate in International Relations from the University of Pennsylvania. Over the years his more than fifty articles and monographs have appeared in such publications as *Sh'ma*, the *Jerusalem Letter*, and the *Journal of Jewish Communal Service*, in addition to a wide range of anglo-Jewish newspapers, including the *Jewish Journal of Los Angeles*, the *New York Jewish Week*, and *The Forward*. His Pew-funded research on the major national Jewish community relations agencies appeared in a recent publication, *Jewish Polity and American Civil Society: Communal Agencies and Religious Movements in the American Public Square* (Lanham, MD: Rowman & Littlefield, 2002). In 2004, he produced a textbook on the practice of Jewish community relations, entitled *You Shall Not Stand Idly By*, published by the American Jewish Committee. In early 2005, Dr. Windmueller collaborated with Professor Gerald Bubis in producing the first study on the formation of the UJC (United Jewish Communities), entitled *Predictability to Chaos?? How American Jewish Leaders Reinvented their National Jewish Communal System*. In addition, he is writing about Jewish political behavior, having released several studies on Jewish voting patterns, including a major study entitled "Are American Jews Becoming Republican: Insights into Jewish Political Behavior," which was released by the Jerusalem Center for Public Affairs.

**FRED ZEIDMAN** is Chairman Emeritus of the United States Holocaust Memorial Council, appointed by President George W. Bush in March 2002 and serving in that position from 2002–10. Fred Zeidman also serves as Chairman Emeritus of the University of Texas Health Science System Houston. He is a prominent Houston based business and civic leader and is on the Board of the Memorial Hermann Hospital. He further serves on the Board of Directors and Executive Committee of the University of Saint Thomas and Houston Community College Foundation. Mr. Zeidman is Chairman of the Board of Petroflow Energy and a Director of Hyperdynamics Corp., Lucas Energy Inc., Straight Path Communications Inc., Petro River Oil and Prosperity Bank in Houston. Mr. Zeidman is National Chairman of Israel Bonds, member of the Executive Committee and Chairman of the Audit Committee of the Jewish National Fund, (JNF) and on the Board of American Friends of Yad Vashem. He is Vice Chairman of the Republican Jewish Coalition, and has played a leadership role in many other organizations. He also serves as Board of trustee and Member of the Executive Committee of the National World War II Museum in New Orleans. He served on the U.S. Delegation to the Anti-Semitism Conference in Berlin. Mr. Zeidman holds a Bachelor's degree from Washington University in St. Louis and a Master's in Business Administration from New York University.

**BRUCE ZUCKERMAN** is the Myron and Marian Casden Director of the Casden Institute and a Professor of Religion at USC, where he teaches courses in the Hebrew Bible, the Bible in western literature, the ancient Near East, and archaeology. A specialist in photographing and reconstructing ancient texts, he is involved in numerous projects related to the Dead Sea Scrolls. On ancient topics, his major publications are *Job the Silent: A Study in Biblical Counterpoint* (New York: Oxford Univ., 1991) and

*The Leningrad Codex: A Facsimile Edition* (Grand Rapids, MI: Eerdmans; Leiden: Brill, 1998), for which he and his brother Kenneth did the principal photography. Zuckerman also has a continuing interest in modern Jewish thought, often looking at modern issues from an ancient perspective. He most recently co-authored *Double Takes: Thinking and Rethinking Issues of Modern Judaism in Ancient Contexts* (Lanham: MD: Univ. Press of America) with Zev Garber and contributed a chapter to Garber's book, *Mel Gibson's Passion: The Film, the Controversy, and Its Implications* (West Lafayette, IN: Purdue Univ., 2006).

# The USC Casden Institute for the Study of the Jewish Role in American Life

The American Jewish community has played a vital role in shaping the politics, culture, commerce and multiethnic character of Southern California and the American West. Beginning in the mid-nineteenth century, when entrepreneurs like Isaias Hellman, Levi Strauss and Adolph Sutro first ventured out West, American Jews became a major force in the establishment and development of the budding Western territories. Since 1970, the number of Jews in the West has more than tripled. This dramatic demographic shift has made California—specifically, Los Angeles—home to the second largest Jewish population in the United States. Paralleling this shifting pattern of migration, Jewish voices in the West are today among the most prominent anywhere in the United States. Largely migrating from Eastern Europe, the Middle East and the East Coast of the United States, Jews have invigorated the West, where they exert a considerable presence in every sector of the economy—most notably in the media and the arts. With the emergence of Los Angeles as a world capital in entertainment and communications, the Jewish perspective and experience in the region are being amplified further. From artists and activists to scholars and professionals, Jews are significantly influencing the shape of things to come in the West and across the United States. In recognition of these important demographic and societal changes, in 1998 the University of Southern California established a scholarly institute dedicated to studying contemporary Jewish life in America with special emphasis on the western United States. The Casden Institute explores issues related to the interface between the Jewish community and the broader, multifaceted cultures that form the nation—issues of relationship as much as of Jewishness itself. It is also enhancing the educational experience for students at USC and elsewhere by exposing them to the problems—and promise—of life in Los Angeles' ethnically, socially, culturally and economically diverse community. Scholars, students and community leaders examine the ongoing contributions of American Jews in the arts, business, media, literature, education, politics, law and social relations, as well as the relationships between Jewish Americans and other groups, including African Americans,

Latinos, Asian Americans and Arab Americans. The Casden Institute's scholarly orientation and contemporary focus, combined with its location on the West Coast, set it apart from—and makes it an important complement to—the many excellent Jewish Studies programs across the nation that center on Judaism from an historical or religious perspective.

For more information about the USC Casden Institute,
visit www.usc.edu/casdeninstitute, e-mail casden@usc.edu,
or call (213) 740-3405.